RAILWAYS OF IRELAND

C. Winchester

AMBERLEY

First published 2014

Amberley Publishing
The Hill, Stroud
Gloucestershire, GL5 4EP

www.amberley-books.com

Copyright © C. Winchester, 2014

The right of C. Winchester to be identified as the Author of this work has been asserted in accordance with the Copyrights, Designs and Patents Act 1988.

ISBN 978 1 4456 4039 6 (print)
ISBN 978 1 4456 4072 3 (ebook)

All rights reserved. No part of this book may be reprinted or reproduced or utilised in any form or by any electronic, mechanical or other means, now known or hereafter invented, including photocopying and recording, or in any information storage or retrieval system, without the permission in writing from the Publishers.

British Library Cataloguing in Publication Data.
A catalogue record for this book is available from the British Library.

Typeset in 9.5pt on 12pt Celeste.
Typesetting by Amberley Publishing.
Printed in the UK.

Contents

Introduction to This Edition   5

Ireland's Railway Systems   7

The Image Archive   31

Ireland – Gem of the Sea   78

Touring for Health and Pleasure   79

Acknowledgements   95

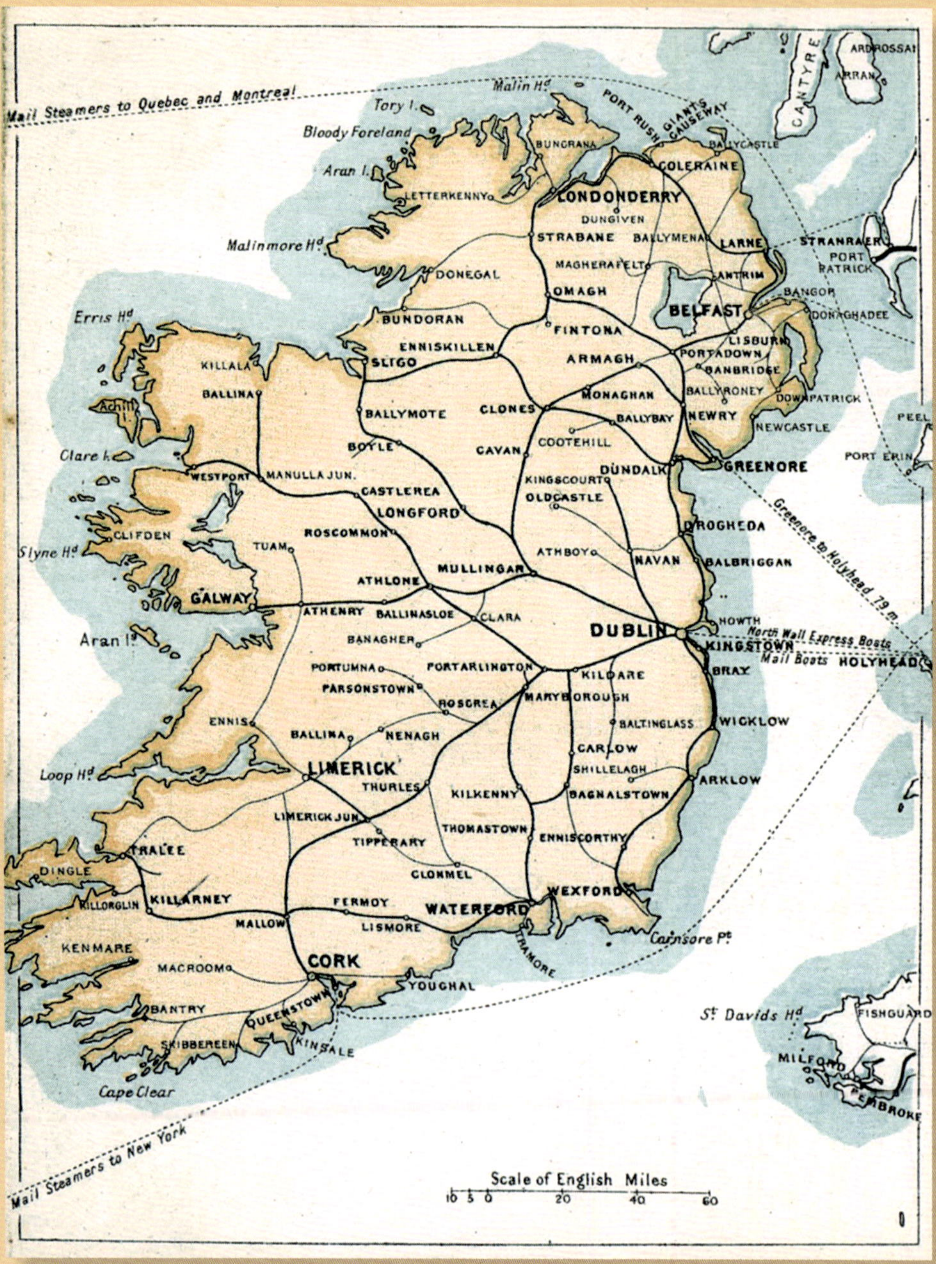

Mail Steamers to Quebec and Montreal
Malin Hd
Tory I.
Bloody Foreland
Aran I.
PORT RUSH
GIANT'S CAUSEWAY
BALLYCASTLE
CANTYRE
ARDROSSAN
ARRAN
BUNCRANA
COLERAINE
LETTERKENNY
LONDONDERRY
DUNGIVEN
STRABANE
BALLYMENA
LARNE
STRANRAER
PORT PATRICK
Malinmore Hd
DONEGAL
MAGHERAFELT
ANTRIM
OMAGH
BANGOR
BELFAST
DONAGHADEE
Erris Hd
BUNDORAN
FINTONA
ENNISKILLEN
LISBURN
PORTADOWN
KILLALA
SLIGO
ARMAGH
BANBRIDGE
BALLINA
BALLYRONEY
MONAGHAN
DOWNPATRICK
Achill
BALLYMOTE
CLONES
BALLYBAY
NEWRY
PEEL
NEWCASTLE
Clare I.
BOYLE
CAVAN
COOTEHILL
GREENORE
PORT ERIN
DUNDALK
WESTPORT
MANULLA JUN.
KINGSCOURT
CASTLEREA
OLDCASTLE
LONGFORD
Greenore to Holyhead 79 m.
CLIFDEN
ROSCOMMON
DROGHEDA
Slyne Hd
TUAM
ATHBOY
NAVAN
BALBRIGGAN
MULLINGAR
ATHLONE
GALWAY
ATHENRY
BALLINASLOE
CLARA
HOWTH
DUBLIN
North Wall Express Boats
Aran Is.
BANAGHER
KINGSTOWN
Mail Boats
HOLYHEAD
PORTUMNA
PORTARLINGTON
KILDARE
BRAY
PARSONSTOWN
ROSCREA
MARYBOROUGH
ENNIS
BALTINGLASS
WICKLOW
BALLINA
NENAGH
CARLOW
Loop Hd
LIMERICK
SHILLELAGH
THURLES
KILKENNY
BAGNALSTOWN
ARKLOW
LIMERICK JUN.
TIPPERARY
THOMASTOWN
ENNISCORTHY
TRALEE
DINGLE
CLONMEL
KILLARNEY
KILLORGLIN
FERMOY
WEXFORD
MALLOW
WATERFORD
LISMORE
TRAMORE
Carnsore Pt.
KENMARE
CORK
MACROOM
YOUGHAL
BANTRY
QUEENSTOWN
St. Davids Hd
FISHGUARD
SKIBBEREEN
KINSALE
MILFORD
PEMBROKE
Cape Clear
Mail Steamers to New York
Scale of English Miles
10 5 0
20
40
60

Introduction to This Edition

The main text of this book comes from the *Railway Wonders of the World* which was edited and largely written by Clarence Winchester, who also produced similar volumes on aircraft and shipping. It was originally published as weekly parts issued from 1935 to 1936, and subsequently bound in two large volumes. It provides a fascinating period perspective on Ireland's Railways at an important transition period in their development. As Winchester states, 'From the beginning of the railways until today railway conditions in Ireland have been different from those in England, Scotland and Wales'. Those conditions saw many individual companies spreading the rails across the Ireland and this resulted in a number of different gauges. The main Irish gauge was 5 feet 3 inches, although there were and are many examples of narrower gauges. Gradually the companies were amalgamated to form bigger concerns, most notably with the railway companies within the Irish Free State being combined in 1925 into the Great Southern Railways. By the mid-1930s Winchester was able to list four principal railways in Ireland: The Great Southern Railways, the Great Northern Railway, the Northern Counties Committee (LMS) and the Belfast & County Down Railway.

To celebrate the 180th anniversary of the opening of Ireland's first railway, the Dublin & Kingstown Railway of 1834 – incidentally built to the English gauge of 4 feet 8.5 inches even though it was partially engineered by Isambard Kingdom Brunel who had championed his own broad gauge of just over 7 feet for the GWR – we are republishing Clarence Winchester's account. It is accompanied with a new selection of photographs of the railways, drawn from a number of sources which are acknowledged at the end of this book.

John Christopher, editor

Great Southern & Western Railway route map, published in *The Sunny Side of Ireland*, 1902.

Map published in the 1930s showing a total mileage of around 3,000 miles.

Ireland's Railway Systems

From Small Beginnings to Great Achievements

From the beginning of the railways until today railway conditions in Ireland have been different from those in England, Scotland and Wales. The first railways in Ireland were built to carry passengers rather than goods, because there was neither heavy mineral traffic nor a big output of manufactured articles to transport. Since the first railway was opened in 1834 the population has declined from about eight millions to little over half that number.

Most of the larger towns are on the coast or on navigable rivers, so that cheap transport by water is available. In recent years the railways have paid attention to road transport, and have co-ordinated and developed road auxiliary services for goods and passengers.

There are four principal railways – the Great Southern Railways, the Great Northern Railway (Ireland), the Northern Counties Committee (London Midland and Scottish Railway), and the Belfast and County Down Railway. Most of the Irish main lines are on the 5 ft 3 in. gauge.

The railways which were entirely within the Irish Free State were combined on January 1, 1925, into the Great Southern Railways, which, at the time of writing, operate 2,157 miles of 5 ft 3 in. track. The Great Northern Railway, however, extends on both sides of the border, having a total of 562 miles of track, of which 332 miles, or 59 per cent, are in Northern Ireland; the gauge is 5 ft 3 in. The Northern Counties Committee (London Midland and Scottish Railway), which operates in Northern Ireland, has 201 miles of 5 ft 3 in. track and 64 miles of 3 ft gauge.

The standard gauge of 4 ft 8½ in. is not used in Ireland. During the war of 1914–18, when English rolling-stock was used in France, the Irish stock could not be requisitioned because of this difference. The Irish gauge of 5 ft 3 in. is found also in the States of Victoria and South Australia, and in Brazil.

Railways have been operated in Ireland for more than a century, the first railway being the Dublin and Kingstown Railway, which was opened to the public on December 17, 1834. It connected the capital with the port of Kingstown, now called Dun Laoghaire, and was about six miles in length.

The project had to overcome considerable opposition. One opponent, Mr O'Hanlon, told a Railway Committee of the House of Commons in 1833 that it 'would be a monstrous thing that the solid advantages of commerce, manufactures, and all the blessings resulting therefrom, should be sacrificed to a few nursery maids descending from the town of Kingstown to the sea at Dunleary, to perform the pleasures of ablution.'

Kingstown, originally called Dunleary, was at one time a fishing village. But the mouth of the River Liffey became choked with sandbanks that made the approach to Dublin very difficult for vessels of any size. Therefore a harbour was built by the engineer Rennie, who began work in 1816, and the place was named Kingstown when George IV visited Ireland in 1821.

The contractor who undertook the construction of the railway became a national character. He was William Dargan, and he was described as a 'prompt, sagacious and far-seeing man,' who judged character by instinct and was seldom mistaken in those whom he selected to carry out his plans. He had been engaged under the engineer, Thomas Telford, on the construction of the Holyhead Road, and returned to Ireland, where he became a contractor. He was known as 'the workman's friend,' because of the justice and fairness with which he dealt with his employees, and he was also spoken of as 'the man with his hand in his pocket,' because of his open-handed generosity. He had 2,000 men working on the construction of Ireland's first railway, and he was afterwards a part-contractor for some of the lines now absorbed in the Great Southern system. Towards the close of his life he became one of the wealthiest men in Ireland; but, partly through his own generosity and partly because of the failure of companies in which his money was invested, he died in penury. His name is perpetuated by a tablet on the National Gallery in, Dublin, which is inscribed:

'National Gallery of Ireland. Founded A.D. *1864*. Erected by the fellow-countrymen of William Dargan Esquire, aided by the Imperial Government, in commemoration of his munificent liberality in founding and sustaining the Dublin Industrial Exhibition of *1853*.' Thus there is a connexion between Ireland's first railway and her National Gallery.

The Dublin and Kingstown Railway was intended to be opened in June, 1834, but there was a delay owing to many difficulties. A few days after the permanent way had been completed a storm of exceptional violence demolished the bridge across the Dodder at Lansdowne Road.

In September *The Dublin Penny Magazine* announced:

The Railway will be opened on the 18th of the present month. His Excellency the Lord Lieutenant, several noblemen, members of Parliament, and a number of gentlemen have notified their intention of being present on the occasion. We have heard that there will be on the road fifty carriages, and six locomotive engines such as that shown in the engraving, which will convey one thousand persons who have been particularly invited for the occasion.

The first railway in Ireland, the Dublin & Kingstown Railway, passing Merrion on the journey to Kingstown. Four distinct class of carriages are shown with varying degrees of comfort. The line opened in 1834 and had been built to the English standard gauge of 4 feet 8.5 inches.

A Successful Trial

There appears to have been a hitch, as the first trials were not made until October 4, when the steam engine *Vauxhall*, with a small train of carriages 'filled with ladies and gentlemen' travelled from Dublin to the Martello Tower, Williamstown, a distance of 2½ miles. The trip was made four times in either direction, at a speed of 31 miles an hour. The passengers were delighted with the comfort, and some said they could read and write with ease while moving at 'this great speed'.

On the next day the *Hibernia* drew the train to Salthill in sixteen minutes, 'notwithstanding the many difficulties attendant on a first starting.' A journalist, anticipating the success of the railway, penned the following purple passage:

> Hurried by the invisible but stupendous energy of steam the astonished passenger will now glide like Asmodeus over the summits of houses - then skim across the surface of the sea, and, taking shelter under the cliffs, coast among the marine villas and through rocky excavations until he finds himself in the centre of a vast port.

The gauge was the English standard of 4 ft 8½ in. The engines were imported from England, but most of the carriages were the work of Dublin coachbuilders. The rails were of iron, and the sleepers were hewn out of Donnybrook granite. The engineers consulted included George Stephenson, Thomas Telford, Alexander Nimmo, Charles Vignoles, and William Fairburn.

The line was opened on December 17, 1834, and the *Dublin Evening Post* published the following account:

This splendid work was yesterday opened to the public for the regular transmission of passengers to and from Kingstown and the immediate stage of the Black Rock.

Notwithstanding the early hour at which the first train started - half-past nine o'clock - the carriages were filled by a very fashionable concourse of persons, and the greatest eagerness was manifested to witness the first operations of the work.

Up to a quarter-past five the line of road from Merrion to Salt Hill was thronged with spectators, who loudly cheered each train that passed them. The average rate at which the trip was performed yesterday was nineteen minutes and a half, including the delay of about two minutes at the Rock, where passengers were taken up. Much confusion was occasioned at starting by the want of proper arrangement, but this inconvenience will be very easily obviated.

The utmost precautions were, however, taken to prevent the possibility of accident by stationing men at proper intervals along the road, and the trains at starting were propelled slowly for a short distance for the same object. Although there could not have been less than from three to four thousand persons upon the railway during the day, we are happy to state that these very necessary precautions were attended with the desired effect.

'The carriages started every hour during the day from either point of the line,' stated *Saunders' News-Letter*, reporting the event.

The number of persons desirous to travel by the new conveyance was so great that a vast number of persons were not fortunate enough to secure a seat. The average time in which each trip was made varied from fifteen to twenty minutes; but it is to be considered that more than the usual number of carriages were attached to each engine in order to afford greater accommodation.

Four Classes

The carriages were of four classes: first, second, closed second, and third. A contemporary account stated: 'The railway coaches of the first and second class may be almost called elegant; the third-class carriages are superior to those in use on the English railways.'

The locomotive *Hibernia* was designed by Richard Roberts, of Sharp, Roberts & Company, who established works in Manchester in 1833 for the manufacture of locomotives. It had a single pair of driving wheels, 5 ft in diameter, and a pair of leading wheels 3 ft in diameter. Although a horizontal boiler working at a pressure of 75 lb was adopted, the cylinders were mounted vertically over the centre line of the leading axle. They were 11 in. in diameter by 16 in. stroke, and the power was transmitted through connecting rods and bell-cranks, with arms of equal length, to the driving wheels. The valve motion was likewise original; there were no eccentrics, but short arms on the bell-cranks for the movement of rocking shafts near the foot-plate.

Three locomotives of this type were built; but they proved a failure, the bell-cranks, through not being a good mechanical job, being the weak feature. Beyond these three engines for Ireland only one other of this design was built. This was the *Experiment* for the Liverpool & Manchester Railway.

When the extension of one and three-quarter miles to Dalkey was completed it was operated by atmospheric traction until 1856, when it was converted to steam operation. In that year the line was leased to the railway then known as the Waterford, Wexford, Wicklow, & Dublin Railway, for £36,000 a year.

Although the original line from Dublin to Kingstown was only six miles long, it cost over £300,000, and was therefore among the most expensive of the early railways. Despite this, the Dublin & Kingstown Railway, which has long since been incorporated in the Great Southern system, was a paying concern, dividends as high as 10 per cent being paid for the year ended March 31, 1846.

One of the first steam locomotives in Ireland, *Hibernia* was designed by Richard Roberts of Manchester. It featured a single driving wheel of 5-foot diameter, and a leading wheel 3 feet in diameter.

In comparison with England railway construction in Ireland was slow. The next line to be opened was in 1839, when the Ulster Railway Company opened a railway from Belfast to Lisburn, about seven miles, and extended it in 1841 to Portadown, and in 1848 to Armagh. This railway was afterwards incorporated in the Great Northern. The Dublin & Drogheda Railway, which was much more ambitious as to length, was opened on May 24, 1844. Amiens Street Station was to be the Dublin terminus, but the first train did not begin its journey of nearly thirty-two miles from the station, for the reason that the bridge across the Royal Canal had not been completed. This was a set-back, but not of sufficient seriousness to delay the opening. A temporary platform was built on the other side of the canal, and the Lord Lieutenant of that time, Earl de Grey, arrived with his suite, and declared the railway open for passenger traffic. He then entered one of the seven carriages, and made the journey to Drogheda.

The time for the thirty-two miles was one hour eighteen minutes, the return journey being made in five minutes less than the outward one. Express trains now cover the distance in little over 'even time'. Wherever coastguards were available they were stationed along the line, to salute the train as it went by. 'Not the slightest accident occurred,' a newspaper of the time proudly announced. The previous day, to make sure of the line before they invited the Lord Lieutenant to ride on their railway, the shareholders and their friends made a trial trip of their own and celebrated the occasion by a 'sumptuous entertainment'.

By 1845 the three railways of Ireland covered a total of only seventy miles, compared with about 1,700 miles in Great Britain. In 1847 one of the worst disasters in the economic history of Ireland, the Great Famine, occurred. The earnings of the railway companies fell considerably. English capitalists were chary of investing in Irish railways, and work on new lines was held up by the lack of money. After the Great Famine, however, the work of building railways proceeded, and every year saw further lengths of line opened to traffic.

The first three railways had lines of three different gauges, the dimensions being: Dublin & Kingstown Railway, 4 ft 8½ in.; Ulster Railway, 6 ft 2 in.; Dublin & Drogheda Railway, 5 ft 3 in. According to one legend, the engineers of the Ulster Railway and those of the Dublin & Drogheda line deliberately planned the tracks on different gauges, so that if two lines ever met, neither company could use the rolling-stock of the other.

A Royal Commission was set up to report on the muddle, with the result that the width of the Irish gauge was fixed at 5 ft 3 in. The gauge of the Ulster Railway was altered about 1846, and that of the Dublin & Kingstown Railway in 1857, the alteration costing the latter company £38,000.

The construction of the early railways was a task of considerable magnitude. For example, on the Londonderry and Coleraine line it was decided, in 1846, to blow a hill, through which a tunnel had been begun, into the sea. A heading or gallery was hewn in the rock from the side of the cliff, 50 ft in length, at the end of which a shaft was sunk for 22 ft to the level of the railway. Another gallery was made at the bottom, running at right angles to the first one, and farther into the rock. At the end of this was placed a charge of 2,400 pounds of powder, the earth was filled in, and the electric wires were arranged. A small charge of 600 pounds of powder was then placed higher up in the rock. When the explosion took place a huge mass of rock, estimated at something like 30,000 tons, rolled into the sea.

The famous engineer, I. K. Brunel, whose name is more particularly associated with the history of the Great Western Railway, did not confine his attention to England. Possibly his most spectacular work was carried out on a stretch of line between Bray and Wicklow, some 16 miles in length. It was said the Bray Head could not be conquered, and Brunel accepted the challenge. At one point south of Bray he bridged a wild ravine with a wooden viaduct 300 ft long and 75 ft high. Before it was quite finished it was destroyed in a night by the sea, and another was built. A few years later a train was derailed while crossing. It was found that the waves had battered the piers of the viaduct with such force that the vibration of the whole structure had thrown the rails out of gauge, and the viaduct was abandoned. In places the line was on a ledge 70 ft above the sea, enclosed here and there by a roof to protect the track from stones falling from the heights above it. The line was very costly to maintain, £40,000 being spent in 10 years on defence works, and the shareholders did not appreciate Brunel's spectacular achievement, which was so costly to maintain against the elements.

In the early days the Irish railways were somewhat haphazard. There is a story that on one line some locomotives were altered from tender engines to tank engines, and that the brakes of this type, which were on the tenders, had disappeared in the process of alteration. When the driver wished to stop a train, having no brakes on his engine, he whistled. The guard heard the whistle and then applied the brakes.

An accident with a terrible death-roll occurred on June 12, 1889, at Armagh, when eighty passengers lost their lives. An excursion train, crammed with school children and teachers, was on its way to the seaside resort of Warrenpoint. The engine was not powerful enough to pull the train up an incline, and it stopped on 'dead centre', that is to say, with both its pistons wrongly placed for re-starting. The driver divided the train into two parts, 'scotching' the wheels of the rear part with stones to prevent it from running downhill. He intended to take the first part of the train to the top of the incline, and then return for the second part. To get over the difficulty caused by having stopped on 'dead centre', he backed the first part of the train. This struck the uncoupled back section, which jolted the stones away and began to slip down the incline, at the bottom of which was an ordinary train.

It is said that some passengers were in the guard's van of this section, and that, in an attempt to help the guard by applying the hand brake, they turned the handle the wrong way, releasing the brake instead of applying it. The carriages gathered speed and went faster and faster down the incline, until they crashed into the other train, with terrible results. Except for the Quintinshill accident in 1915, which involved an estimated death-roll of 224 passengers and three railway servants, the Armagh collision was the worst disaster in the history of the railways of the United Kingdom.

On the morning of 9 August 1867 the Enniscorthy to Dublin train was derailed on a viaduct at Bray Head. Two people were killed in the accident, another twenty-five injured. Opened in October 1855 the Wicklow & Wexford Railway had been surveyed and engineered by Isambard Kingdom Brunel, but the cliff-face line became known in the area as 'Brunel's Folly' because of the difficulties and expense in maintaining it. After the accident the timber viaduct remained in use until 1876 when the line was diverted inland.

But in spite of this terrible accident, the Irish railways have always been noted for their efficient operation.

During the various 'troubles' the railways suffered considerably from all parties. In the Easter Rising of 1916, stations in Dublin were taken over by the Irish Volunteers, but were evacuated. Then the military authorities restricted passenger traffic and used some of the stations as barracks. The permanent way was blown up in several places and a cattle train was derailed. On one occasion an engine was set running uncontrolled over a section of the line, but was thrown off before any damage was done. The curfew law in Dublin, Cork, and Belfast limited suburban evening traffic, and from time to time there were strikes and boycotts. Certain areas were closed by the authorities and markets were stopped, so that the railways lost passenger and goods traffic, and, in addition, certain lines were closed altogether.

During the Civil War in 1922 rails were torn up, bridges destroyed, and trains derailed or fired upon. A Railway Protection, Repair, and Maintenance Corps was formed, temporary repairs were made, blockhouses were set up along the lines, and armoured trains were run. Indeed, few railways have had so many difficulties with which to contend as those of Ireland.

The Largest System

The Great Southern is the largest railway in Ireland, its route mileage – all in the Free State – being nearly three times as much as that of the other three important railways. It employs 12,044 out of the 15,420 railway workers whose headquarters are in the Free State. It took over no fewer than twenty-six lines when it came into being in January, 1925. Among the companies absorbed were the Great Southern & Western, the Midland Great Western, and the Dublin & South Eastern. The main routes from Dublin are to Limerick Junction, Mallow, and Cork; to Mullingar and Galway; and to Wicklow and Waterford. The mail steamers from Holyhead arrive at Kingstown (Dun Laoghaire), whence through carriages are worked in connexion with the mail steamers to Cork and Queenstown (Cobh). In connexion with the steamers from Fishguard to Rosslare Harbour, through trains are run from Rosslare Harbour to Waterford and Cork.

The line running south from Dublin passes the frequented seaside resort of Bray (Bri Chualann), which is also a centre from which to explore the beauties of County Wicklow, 'the Garden of Ireland.' Farther on, beyond Greystones, is the picturesque town of Wicklow. The Devil's Glen, a lovely mountain pass, is near. After Wicklow the line leaves the coast and runs via Rathdrum to Avoca, near the 'Meeting of the Waters', about which Thomas Moore, the Irish poet, wrote a song. Avoca and Woodenbridge, just beyond it, are in the heart of delightful country. The railway goes on through the old town of Arklow to Macmine Junction. Hence one line runs south-east to Wexford and Rosslare Harbour, and another west via New Ross to Waterford. Waterford was once a Danish town named Vedrifiord, 'the Star of the Suir.'

Another route from Dublin to Waterford goes through Kildare, Portarlington, Maryborough, and Kilkenny: while between these two routes is a web of connecting lines. West from Waterford the network of lines covers the south-west of Ireland.

Cork city is the centre for the tourist who wishes to see this part of the country, and it is served by lines branching out in all directions. Cobh (Queenstown), the Atlantic port, is one of the terminals of the Great Southern. A line runs east from Cork to Youghal, from which port Sir Walter Ralegh, its mayor, sailed to found Virginia. To the north a line runs parallel with this one, connecting Mallow and Waterford, and tapping beautiful country. South-west from Cork a line, with a number of branches to the coast, runs to Bantry, through Bandon. From Mallow a line runs westward, branching south to Kenmare, and west to Killarney, to Tralee, and to Valencia. From Tralee a line goes through the Dingle peninsula. Another branch runs from Tralee through Listowel to Limerick city, the third town in the Free State. The power station of the Shannon Electricity Scheme is situated at Ardnacrusha, three miles away, from which radiates the network of high-tension cables carrying current to all parts of the country.

From Limerick a line runs to Ennis, the chief town in County Clare, which is a junction, one railway going west and then south along the coast, and the other going north to Athenry (for Galway), Claremorris, and Sligo. The cliff scenery all along the coast-line from Ennis is magnificent, culminating in grandeur in the Cliffs of Moher, near Lahinch. This line branches at Moyasta, one track running west to the bathing resort of Kilkee, and the other east to Kilrush, on the estuary of the Shannon.

Galway, with its fine harbour, on the west coast, is reached from Dublin by the main line that crosses the Central Plain of Ireland. The town's records go back to 1124, and many Anglo-Norman families settled here. The port had an important trade with France and Spain, and some of the old houses have a foreign appearance. One building, the Lynch Mansion, now a bank, has a strange story. The only son of the mayor of the town, in 1524, stabbed the son of his Spanish visitor in jealousy, and gave himself up to justice. The mayor sentenced him to death, but no executioner could be found. The mayor executed his only son, hanging him from the window with his own hand.

The Aran Islands, reached by steamer from Galway, are attractive, the islanders being people with a character of their own, and might be a race apart from those on the mainland.

The line runs west into Connemara from Galway, the train journey being a revelation of successive scenes of beauty - mountains, lakes, and rivers. The Twelve Bens, seen from the train, form a glorious group. Recess, which is 163 miles from Dublin, is one of the choicest spots in Connemara, and is a centre for anglers and tourists. Its lough is one and a half miles long, and is ornamented on the south bank by the plantations of Glendalough House. The train

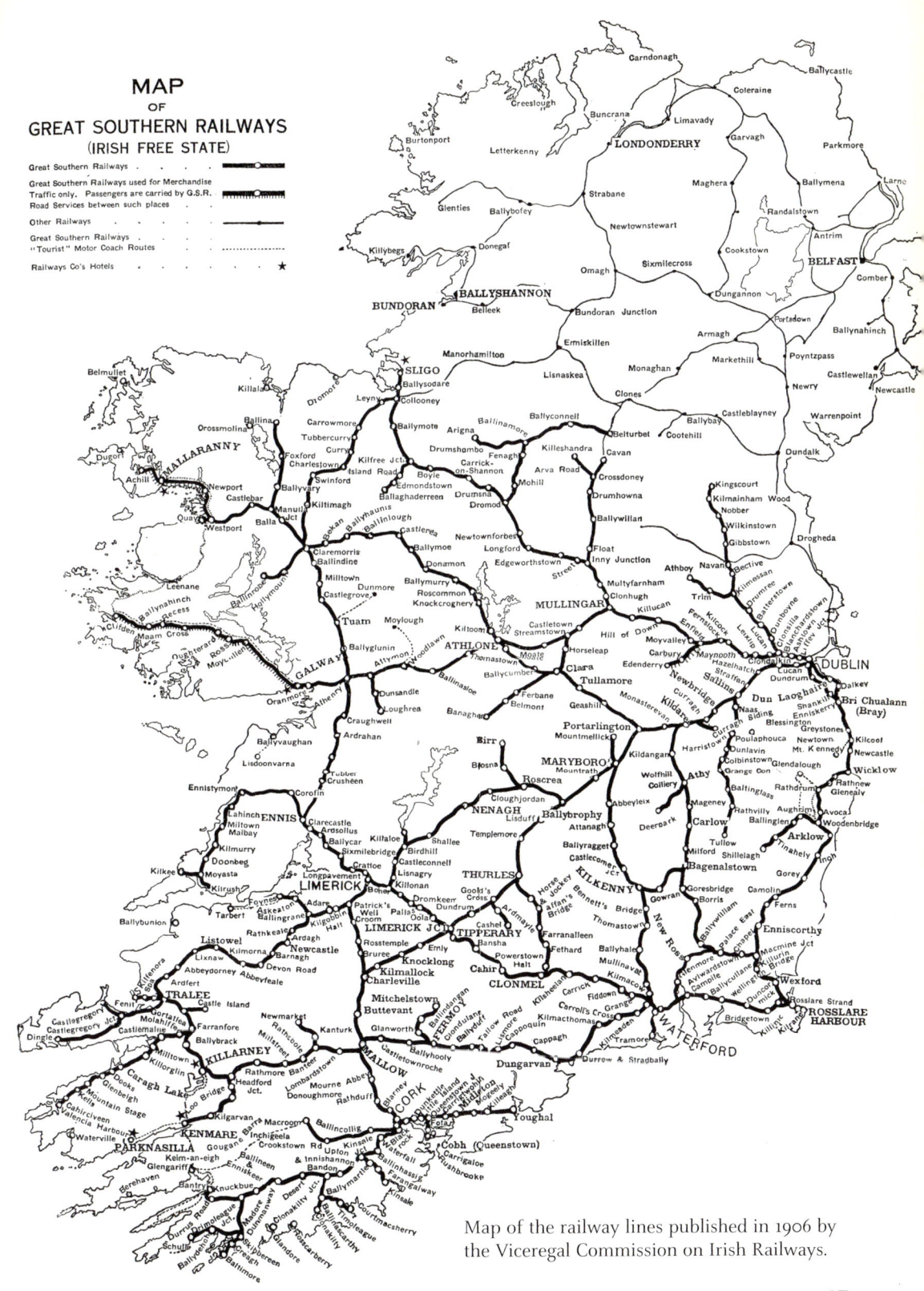

Map of the railway lines published in 1906 by the Viceregal Commission on Irish Railways.

17

skirts Lough Glendalough, and the aspect of Glen Inagh and the Twelve Bens is very fine as it approaches the foot of Derryclare Lough. The line trends south-west, and passes Athry Lough, but then resumes its westward course to the south of Ballynahinch Lough, across which the Twelve Bens show to great advantage. The country now becomes wild and rugged as the train steams towards Clifden, and its wildness is the more marked after the picturesque combination of lake, river, and plantation around Ballynahinch Castle. Clifden is famous as the landing-place of Alcock and Brown, on the first direct Transatlantic flight, in 1919.

The northward continuation of the line from Ennis connects at Athenry with the main line from Dublin to Galway. Beyond Athenry is Claremorris, a junction for a line to Manulla Junction, whence one branch runs West to Westport, Mallaranny, and Achill, and the other north to Ballina. Mallaranny is the headquarters for tourists exploring West Mayo. It is screened from the Atlantic gales by the mountains of the Curraun Promontory. Facing Achill is the largest island on the Irish coast, Achill Island, which has an area of about fifty-five square miles. The rock scenery is splendid.

Sligo, an important seaport, is connected with the western network of railways via Collooney, near the end of the long branch from Limerick, Ennis, and Claremorris.

Central Ireland is served by the sections and branches of the Great Southern system, which extends from Cavan in the north to mid-Tipperary in the south, and from the Boyne in the east to the Shannon in the west. Within the area are included the Bog of Allen, and the great Central Plain of Ireland, which is traversed by the main line of the western section from Dublin to Galway. Mullingar and Athlone, the two principal towns, are important junctions. Athlone, through a branch line from Portarlington links up the western and southern sections. Tara Hill, the valley of the Boyne, Clonmacnois, the Upper Shannon, the Westmeath lakes, and many other places are in this area.

Ballybrophy is the junction for the Birr (Parsonstown) and Roscrea and Nenagh branches. The Roscrea–Nenagh branch gives a connexion from Dublin to Limerick as an alternative to the Limerick Junction route.

Athlone, near which is a powerful radio transmitting station, is almost in the centre of Ireland. It lies on both banks of the Shannon. The railway station is on the west side of the river, the longest in Ireland, which is spanned by a fine railway bridge.

The chief features of the district served by the Meath branch of the western main system are the Boyne Valley and Tara, Trim, Bective, and their surroundings.

The Boyne valley is at its loveliest near Navan. Near Kilmessan Junction, whence a branch line runs to Trim, and Athboy, is the famous Tara Hill. Trim, the county town of Meath, is thirty miles from Dublin. About two miles south of the town is the parish of Laracor, associated with Dean Swift. 'Stella,' chaperoned by Mrs Dingley, lodged at Trim.

Among the early locomotives of the Great Southern is one, No. 36 in the records of the company, of the 'Bury haystack dome' type. It was built by Bury, Curtis, & Kennedy, of Liverpool, in 1848, and incorporated the distinctive design favoured by these builders. It is of the 2-2-2 type, with cylinders

15 in. in diameter by 20 in. stroke. The driving wheels are 6 ft in diameter; the leading and trailing wheels are 4 ft 8 in. and 3 ft 10 in. in diameter respectively. The boiler barrel is 11 ft 11 in. in length between tube-plates, and carries 151 iron tubes of 2 in. external diameter.

The firebox is of copper, fitted with bar crown stays, and screwed iron stays in the water spaces. In addition to the doming of the firebox wrapper-plate, the back-head of the firebox is semicircular. The frames are of the forged bar type, with the cylinders inside, the broad gauge of the Irish railways favouring this arrangement.

The heating surface of the tubes is 1,000 sq. ft, and of the firebox 60 sq. ft, giving an aggregate heating surface of 1,060 sq. ft; the grate area is 12.75 sq. ft. The working pressure is 80 lb per sq. in; and the tractive effort, at 85 per cent of the boiler pressure, is 4,250 lb. The overall length of the engine is 21 ft 2 in., and the height to the rim of the funnel 12 ft 8 in; the centre line of the boiler is 6 ft 4 in. above rail level. The weight is 22 tons 19 cwt.

This locomotive covered 487,919 miles in a quarter of a century of service, being withdrawn from service in January, 1874. The company, then the Great Southern & Western Railway of Ireland, set her upon a pedestal at their locomotive works at Inchicore for permanent preservation as an example of good workmanship.

One of the most interesting inventions of recent years is the Drumm Traction Battery, invented by Dr J. J. Drumm. This battery is used for road and rail transport, and has operated eighty-ton suburban passenger trains on the Great Southern Railways for several years without one failure.

Large-scale track electrification of the Irish railways is not considered an economic possibility, but this quick charging battery was designed to solve the problem. Traffic on the railways is not sufficient to justify the expense of electrification, either by the third rail or the overhead systems. As the distances between the terminal stations of the railways are short compared with those of other countries, it is considered that a Drumm train will be able to cover the longest routes, with a halt of a few minutes for re-charging the batteries at stations about fifty miles apart. Since the inauguration of the Shannon power scheme, plenty of power is available. An economic advantage claimed for the Drumm battery is that its use will reduce the imports of petrol and heavy oil required by petrol-driven and Diesel-engined rail-cars. The battery is a variation of the nickel iron alkaline type.

The original Drumm train was constructed in the Great Southern Railways workshops at Inchicore.

Trial runs in January, 1932, showed that the train could attain a speed of fifty miles an hour within fifty seconds of the start. A speed of fifty-five miles an hour, it is stated, was maintained for the greater part of the journey from Dublin to Bray. The first train was put into commission and a second quickly followed, both becoming part of the Bray–Dublin service. Dr Drumm's invention is one of the most interesting of recent years. Further developments are promised.

The area served by the Great Northern Railway has its full share of historic associations and picturesque scenery. The company links up the Free State with Northern Ireland and was incorporated by an Act of 1877 which amalgamated the four following companies: (i) Dublin & Drogheda Railway, comprising a railway from Dublin to Drogheda, Howth Junction to Howth, and Drogheda to Oldcastle; (2) Dublin & Belfast Junction Railway, comprising a railway from Drogheda to Portadown; (3) Irish North Western Railway, comprising a railway from Dundalk to Enniskillen, which company also worked a line from Enniskillen to Londonderry under lease, and a line from Clones to Cavan; (4) Ulster Railway, comprising a railway from Belfast to Clones, and Portadownto Omagh. Since incorporation the Great Northern has acquired ten other railways, and built four branch lines. The company is a joint owner, with the LMS Railway, of the County Donegal Railways. Connexions are made at Dundalk and Newry with the Dundalk, Newry & Greenore Railway (twenty-seven miles), owned by the LMS but now worked by the Great Northern. It serves a picturesque part of Ireland.

Coast and country are served by the ramifications of the Great Northern. The track runs by the Irish Sea, inland along trout-rippled streams and rich meadows, through orchards that in spring are covered with apple blossoms, by woods of leafy oaks, or over brown bogs, and along winding, island-studded lakes. Westward is Donegal, the Highlands of Ireland, with its kindly, witty people. To the north and east are found the beauties of Enniskillen, Lough Erne, Londonderry, the Giant's Causeway, and the Mountains of an ancient Mourne.

Drogheda is an ancient town which has suffered from warfare, burnings, and pillage. It has reminders of its ancient history in the parts of the old walls that still surround it, while the St Lawrence Gate and the Magdalene Tower are almost perfect.

Armagh, another ancient city which also suffered from warfare, burnings and pillage, is the primatial see in Ireland for the Roman Catholic and Episcopalian Churches. In the olden days it was a centre of education for students from all parts of Europe.

A Frontier Line

The Great Northern Railway forms roughly a gigantic Y, with three of Ireland's chief ports at its three ends: Dublin (with Kingstown), Belfast, and Londonderry. The company claims to have been the first in Great Britain and Ireland, if not in the world, to have its entire passenger rolling-stock lighted by electricity. It claims, also, to be the first company to run restaurant trains in connexion with sporting events and to collect, in one amount, a sum to cover the reserved seat on the train, two meals, and a reserved seat for the sporting event.

In the comparatively small area that it serves, the railway crosses the frontiers and customs barriers of Northern Ireland and the Free State at nine places.

The Great Northern terminus at Dublin is at Amiens Street Station, which covers three and a half acres, and has three platforms. Great Victoria Street Station, Belfast, covers four acres, and has five platforms. At each of the two stations about 2,500,000 passengers are dealt with yearly.

Passengers and mails by the night 'Irish Mail' from London (Euston) and other centres in England via Holyhead, connect at Kingstown Pier with a train to Amiens Street (Dublin), where they are transferred to the morning mail train for Belfast. This train gives a connexion at Dundalk for all stations to Omagh, taking in Carrickmacross, Cootehill, Cavan, and Belturbet branches; at Goraghwood with trains for Newry, Warrenpoint, Armagh, and Banbridge; and at Portadown for Londonderry, via Strabane. Including this train there are five restaurant or buffet car expresses daily in either direction between Dublin and Belfast (112½ miles).

An express leaves Dublin daily in the late afternoon for Belfast, giving connexions at Drogheda for Oldcastle; at Dundalk for Carrickmacross, Cootehill and all stations to Enniskillen and Cavan; at Goraghwood for Newry, Warrenpoint and Banbridge. This train conveys passengers for Scotland via the Belfast and Ardrossan route. Passengers leaving Euston Station (London) by the day 'Irish Mail' and travelling via Holyhead and Kingstown, connect with this train, which enables them to reach Belfast in the evening of the same day.

Travellers by this route to Northern Ireland, and by the afternoon up Limited Mail from Belfast for cross-Channel stations are not troubled by customs examination of their baggage. Through sealed compartments are provided in the trains, as well as on the steamer, and passengers' luggage passes through .the Free State without question.

There is a restaurant car express service between Belfast and Londonderry. The morning mail train from Belfast reaches Londonderry in just over two and a half hours. This train runs in conjunction with the Liverpool, Heysham, and Glasgow cross-Channel steamers, forming a connexion at Portadown with the morning mail from Dublin. In the reverse direction the up express from Londonderry to Belfast carries passengers and mails from Londonderry and stations in the Donegal Highlands, connecting at Portadown with the afternoon up Limited Mail for Dublin and Holyhead.

MIDLAND GREAT
WESTERN RAILWAY
OF
IRELAND
TOURS
IN
CONNEMARA
GALWAY, ACHILL
and West of Ireland
KYLEMORE
(CONNEMARA)
BALLINAHINCH
(CONNEMARA)
CLIFFS OF ACHILL ISLE
LOUGH GILL SLIGO
(CONNEMARA)
F. Hugo d'Alési
FOR ILLUSTRATED TOURIST GUIDES,
or other particulars, apply to MANAGER'S OFFICE.
BROADSTONE STATION, DUBLIN.
IMP. A. BELLIER & Cie PARIS, BORDEAUX

At Dublin there is a heavy seaside traffic with Howth, Malahide, and Skerries, and a frequent service that is increased to a fifteen minutes service on some occasions to carry holiday and residential traffic.

At Belfast the district up to and including Lisburn (eight miles) is residential. The service is half-hourly, except during the rush hours, when trains are run at intervals of from five to ten minutes.

A considerable excursion traffic is carried from all stations during the summer to Bundoran, Warrenpoint, Newcastle, and other places at specially low fares. The excursion fare from Belfast to Warrenpoint and back is only 2s for a total distance of 102 miles. The time occupied for the journey in either direction - little over an hour - is good for excursion trains.

On such occasions as the July Orange Demonstrations, which are held at different places throughout Northern Ireland each year, the railway is called upon to carry some 30,000 additional passengers in a few hours, and this taxes the supply of rolling-stock considerably. Similarly, the annual Trades Holiday on the last Saturday in August causes the exodus of large crowds from Belfast to some selected meeting place on the railway system.

International football matches at Dublin and Belfast attract considerable extra traffic, and express corridor trains are run at cheap fares. The 'Throughout Dining Car Express' is a popular train for Rugby enthusiasts, first-class travel, with luncheon on the outward and dinner on the return journey being provided for a low figure. This express takes slightly over two hours, including a stop for customs examination, to cover the 112½ miles between Dublin and Belfast.

Opposite: Midland Great Western Railway poster for tours in Connemara, Galway, Achill and the west of Ireland, *c.* 1900.

Opposite page, from the top:
The Kestral, a three-cylinder compound engine used on the Great Northern Railway, with one high-pressure cylinder inside and two low-pressure cylinders outside. This 4-4-0 passenger loco of the V class was built by Beyer, peacock & Co. Ltd., of Manchester, for the Great Northern Railway.

A heavy passenger locomotive, this 4-6-0 was employed on the Great Southern system for express work. No. 500 has two cylinders, and is fitted with Walschaerts valve gear. This type of loco hauled the Dublin–Cork mail trains.

4-4-0 Passenger locomotive in service on the Northern Counties Committee, later part of the LMS. This explains why the design recalls the practice of the former Midland Railway of England.

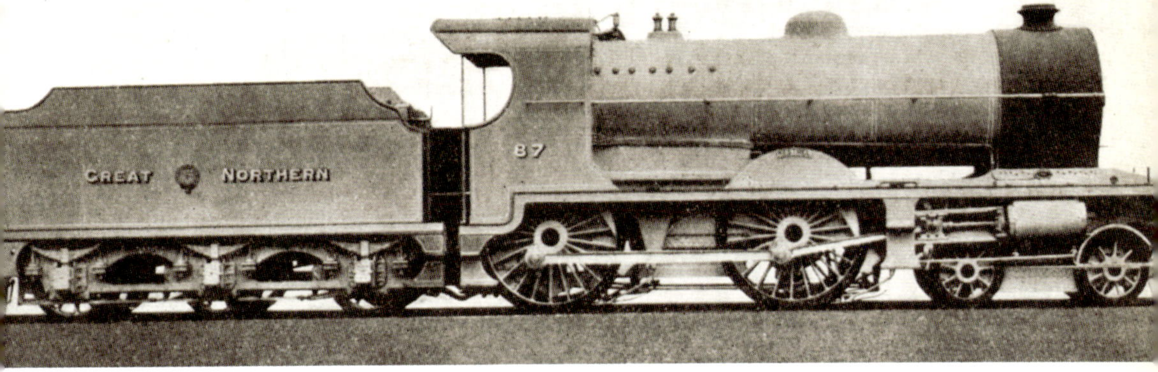
GREAT NORTHERN
87

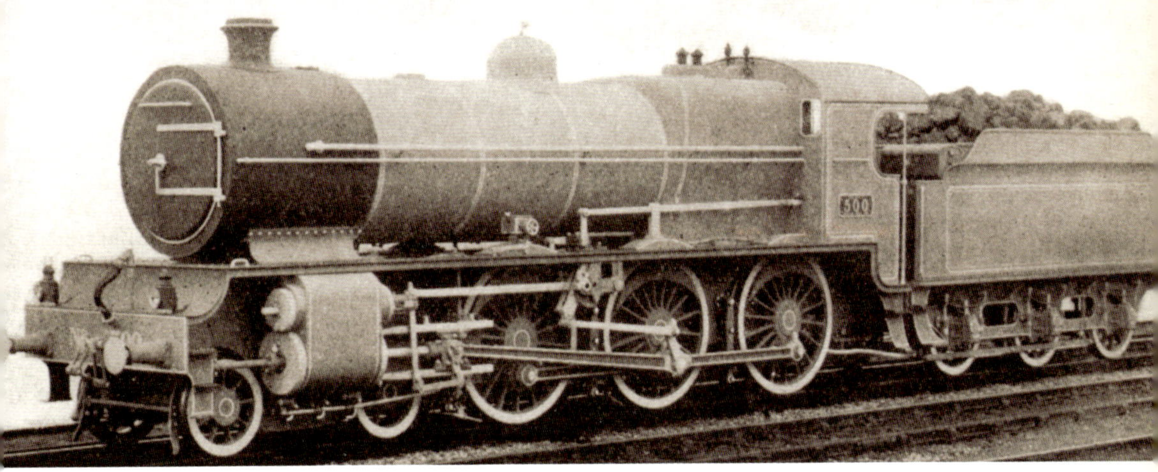
500

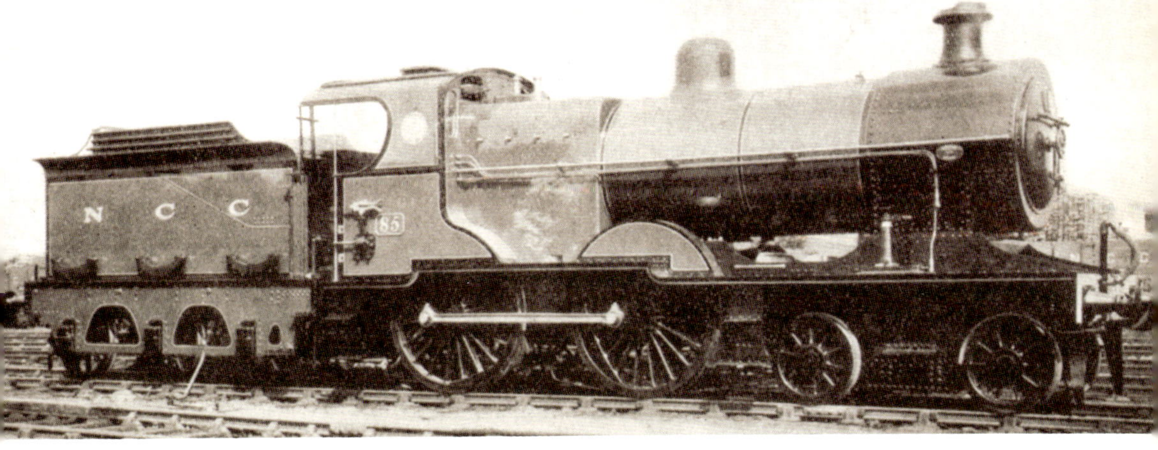
N C C
85

Rail Omnibus Service

The system has connexion at Amiens Street, Dublin, with all sections of the Great Southern Railways for passenger traffic to and from south-western and south-eastern districts. It also connects with the Great Southern at Belturbet, Cavan, and Navan. Enniskillen is the junction for the Sligo, Leitrim & Northern Counties Railway.

At Cookstown and Antrim the services link up with the Northern Counties Committee (LMS); at Strabane with the narrow gauge lines (3 ft) of the County Donegal Joint Committee; and at Londonderry with the Londonderry & Lough Swilly Railway (3 ft gauge). At Newcastle, and Belfast via the Belfast Central Railway, connexions are made with the Belfast & County Down Railway. The Belfast Central line also affords through conveyance of a considerable goods and live stock traffic to and from the Belfast quays with the cross-Channel steamers.

Connexions are also made at Dundalk and Newry with the Dundalk, Newry & Greenore Railway, for the cargo steamships operating between Greenore and Holyhead.

Traffic between Northern Ireland and the Free State is subject to customs examination at the boundary posts. The customs authorities and the railway company have, however, arranged for the examination to take place in the trains. There are boundary posts in Northern Ireland at Goraghwood, Tynan, Newtownbutler, Belleek, and Strabane; and for the Irish Free State at Dundalk, Clones, Monaghan, Pettigo, Ballyshannon and St Johnston.

An innovation on the Great Northern is the pneumatic-tyred rail omnibus, produced by the company's Chief Engineer, Mr G. B. Howden. This vehicle is stated to be the only one of its class in Ireland at the time of writing.

It resembles the ordinary omnibus. The wheels have steel rims interposed between the pneumatic tyre and the rail. The rail omnibus has the advantage over the steam train of being able to stop at level crossings, in addition to stations, to pick up or set down passengers. Besides being more economical to operate in sparsely populated districts, the rail omnibus provides a high degree of comfort.

The main line between Dublin and Belfast is carried over the River Boyne at Drogheda, about thirty-two miles north of Dublin, by the Boyne Viaduct. The structure is about 1,760 ft in length, with fifteen semicircular masonry arch spans, and three girder spans, two of 141 ft and one of 267 ft, the whole being supported on massive masonry piers. The underside of the girders is about 90 ft above high-water level.

The original bridge was built in 1855. The principle of multiple-lattice construction was first applied on a large scale in this bridge. It was rebuilt in 1930–32, to the designs of the Chief Engineer of the Great Northern Railway.

The Northern Counties Committee (London Midland & Scottish Railway) is popularly known as the Northern Counties Railway. It has direct connexions with the parent company in Great Britain by a service of LMS steamers between Stranraer and Larne, and between Heysham and Belfast. The railway serves the counties of Antrim, Londonderry and Tyrone.

The main line runs between the two largest centres of population in Northern Ireland, Belfast (the headquarters and principal terminus) and Londonderry. There are branch lines to Larne Harbour, Ballyclare, Cookstown, Draperstown, Portrush, and Dungiven. Narrow gauge (3 ft) lines between Larne Harbour and Ballymena, with a branch to Ballyclare, between Ballymena and Parkmore, between Bailymoney and Ballvcastle, and between Londonderry and Strabane complete the system. Some branches are closed to passenger traffic.

The district served has many scenic attractions. These include the famous Giant's Causeway; Lough Neagh, the largest lake in the British Isles; the celebrated Antrim Coast Road; the Glens of Antrim; and the Gobbins Cliff Path, said to be the finest marine walk in Europe. The chief industries are associated with the manufacture or linen, and include flax-spinning, weaving, and bleaching. The agricultural interest is of primary importance, flax, grain, and potatoes being extensively produced. Cattle, pigs, and sheep, largely for shipment to Great Britain, are also of importance.

As with many other railways, the Northern Counties has been built up by the amalgamation of a number of small, independent lines. The first section of the system, the Belfast & Ballymena Railway, was opened to Carrickfergus and Ballymena in 1848. The Ballymena, Ballymoney, Coleraine, & Portrush Railway was opened in 1855, and the Londonderry & Coleraine Railway was completed in 1853. Through rail communication between Belfast and Londonderry was, however, not established until the completion of the viaduct over the River Bann at Coleraine in 1860. In 1860 the Belfast & Ballymena Railway became the Belfast & Northern Counties Railway. Next year the Ballymena, Ballymoney, Coleraine & Portrush Railway became amalgamated with it, followed in 1871 by the Londonderry & Coleraine Railway. A number of other railways were amalgamated in later years.

In 1903 the Belfast & Northern Counties Railway was taken over by the Midland Railway of England, and since then its affairs have been administered by the Northern Counties Committee. The Committee comprises members representing the English board and members representing Irish interests. While the line is operated as a distinct concern, and has its own officers and staff, it maintains close association with the directors and chief officers of the London, Midland & Scottish Railway, as the successors of the Midland Railway Company.

Gradients are frequently severe on all sections of the system, but 1 in 80 is seldom exceeded on the broad-gauge lines, although some of the steeper sections are of considerable length. On the narrow-gauge lines 1 in 40 or 1 in 50 is not infrequent, the steepest gradient being 1 in 39 for 1½ miles near Cargan on the Ballymena–Parkmore line. At one point on this line an altitude of 1,250 ft is reached, the highest point attained by railways in Ireland.

There are only two tunnels on the system, both single-line and quite short, one being at Downhill and the other at Whitehead. At Whitehead the tunnel is used by the down trains only, the up trains using the track constructed outside the tunnel when the line was recently doubled between Carrickfergus and Whitehead.

Important engineering features are not lacking, outstanding examples being the loop line at Greenisland and the viaduct over the River Bann at Coleraine.

The Greenisland Loop, between Belfast and Antrim, built in 1931–34, is an avoiding line two and three-quarter miles long, which enables main-line trains to run straight through to and from Belfast without the necessity of proceeding to Greenisland and reversing. The route via Greenisland had always been attended by much delay and expense, owing to the greater distance, the additional locomotives required by reversal, and the gradient encountered immediately after re-starting. These disadvantages were known for more than sixty years and plans were prepared from time to time, but were always abandoned because of the high cost involved. Nothing was done until 1928, when an arrangement was made between the Government of Northern Ireland and the directors of the Northern Counties Committee for the construction of a loop line as an unemployment relief scheme.

The plans were prepared and the entire work was undertaken by the railway, involving an expenditure of £250,000, towards which the Government of Northern Ireland contributed £80,000.

The loop line has a continuous gradient of 1 in 75. It required the excavation of about 240,000 cubic yards of earth and the placing of the earth in new embankments. The maximum cutting is 22 ft and the greatest height of the embankment is 35 ft. The greater part of the line is on a continuous curve, the maximum radius being three-quarters of a mile. The viaduct, which is the largest reinforced concrete railway viaduct in the British Isles, is 630 ft long, and has a maximum height of 70 ft above the level of the stream. The three main arches each have a length of 89 ft. Twenty thousand cubic yards of concrete were placed in bridges and viaducts, one and a quarter miles of new line were constructed, and one and a quarter miles of old line were either raised or lowered. The Loop Line has been compensated for curvature, the minimum radius being sixty chains.

A short distance from the beginning of the new loop line at Whiteabbey there is a wide glen over which the new line had to be carried at a considerable elevation. As the maximum depth was 70 ft a viaduct was necessary, and one of reinforced concrete was built in eighteen months. In addition to the three main arches of 89 ft, there are a number of approach arches on either side of 35 ft span.

Down trains for Larne pass underneath the new loop line at the Belfast end of the main viaduct, so that one line is above the other. This down line crosses the glen at a much lower elevation than the big viaduct, and it is carried by a concrete arch of 89 ft span, with three 35 ft approach arches on either side. The two viaducts and the under-crossing required 17,000 cubic yards of concrete, and 700 tons of mild steel reinforcement, and cost about £65,000.

The new part of the line passes underneath a county road, which is carried on a three-span reinforced concrete bridge, and under one accommodation road, which is carried on a single span concrete bridge. The alteration in the level of the old lines made it possible to eliminate four level crossings by means of one under bridge and two over bridges. On the same section of the line it was also necessary to carry out a road diversion, and provide an under bridge for a district road, which would otherwise have crossed on the level. All these bridges were of reinforced concrete. The earthwork was removed by means of half-yard excavators, which loaded the clay into wagons, in which it was conveyed to the site of the new embankment.

To provide a direct connexion from the north to Larne Harbour for the Stranraer steamer, a single line has been retained from a point half-way along the new loop line to Greenisland.

Colour light signals were installed at Greenisland and Ballyclare Junction, the first station at the end of the new line. The signalling is controlled from a central cabin at Greenisland; and the points at the junction are operated by electric motors. There are electric train indicators in Belfast and Greenisland signal boxes, and there is also an illuminated diagram at Greenisland.

The construction of the loop line, together with minor adjustments made to the crossing loops on the railway north of Ballymena, has reduced the time taken between Belfast and Londonderry by more than twenty minutes and the time between Belfast and Portrush by twenty-five minutes.

Below: Great Southern Railways No. 21. *(J&C McCutcheon Collection)*

The 'North Atlantic Express'

Portrush, in addition to being a seaside resort and golfing centre, is a residential centre for the business and professional people of Belfast.

The River Bann Viaduct, opened in 1924, replaced the original viaduct built in 1860. The new structure consists of eleven spans; five fixed spans on the Coleraine side, the counterweight span, the bascule span, and four fixed spans on the Londonderry side. The bascule span is necessary owing to the shipping trade of Coleraine and is 85 ft from centre to centre of the piers, there being a clear waterway of 70 ft between the fenders built round the piers on either side. The bascule span is of the Strauss type, with underhung counterweight, and is said to be the first example of its kind in the British Isles. It is operated by a special hydraulic system which eliminates friction clutches and provides for reverse operation instead of reversing gears.

The 'North Atlantic Express', instituted after the opening of the Greenisland loop, maintains a daily service between Belfast and Portrush (sixty-five and a quarter miles), and is particularly convenient for Portrush residents whose business interests are in Belfast. This express leaves Portrush in the morning and arrives in Belfast after a run of eighty minutes. The corresponding train from Belfast leaves in the evening on week days, except on Saturdays, when it leaves soon after midday. There is a stop at Ballymena in either direction.

This train is usually hauled by a 4-4-0 express passenger engine recently constructed at the Committee's locomotive works, Belfast. The type is not the most powerful on the system, but it has ample power to maintain the high speeds required. The boiler is of the standard superheated type. The two cylinders are 19 in. diameter by 24 in. stroke, and the driving wheels 6 ft in diameter. The total weight of engine and tender is 84 tons.

The rolling-stock, also built in the Northern Counties workshops, consists of corridor coaches: one 60-ft. Buffet car, one 57-ft brake third, one first, second, and third composite coach, and two third-class coaches, giving a seating capacity of 194.

The body framing of the coaches is of teak, with mahogany panelling outside and inside. The exterior of the train has been designed to give an almost flush finish, and with the large 5-ft windows presents altogether a very attractive appearance.

Above the window in each compartment, and also in the corridors, a sliding extractor ventilator is fitted.

The most powerful Northern Counties locomotives are those designed recently for service in Ireland by Mr W. A. Stainer, Chief Mechanical Engineer of the LMS Railway. These have the 2-6-0 wheel arrangement and conform generally to LMS practice, except that advantage has been taken of the 5 ft 3 in. gauge to widen the firebox. The driving position is on the left side and tip-up seats are provided. The standard tender carries 2,500 gallons of water and five tons of coal.

The Image Archive

GSR No. 236, a class J22 0-6-0. Built by Dubbs in 1895, scrapped in 1951. *(J&C McCutcheon Collection)*

No. 702, at the Inchicore Railway Works. Established in 1844 by the Great Southern & Western Railways, this is still the headquarters for mechanical engineering and rolling stock maintenance for Iarnród Éireann. *(J&C McCutcheon Collection)*

Ex- GS&WR No. 200, a 0-6-0 of the J15 class. *(J&C McCutcheon Collection)*

Midland Great Western Railway express engine *Celtic*, No. 129. *(J&C McCutcheon Collection)*

CIE loco No. 176, J15 class 0-6-0. Built by Sharp Stewart in 1873, scrapped in 1959. *(J&C McCutcheon Collection)*

One of the 2-6-0 two-cylinder superheater engines designed by the LMS which were the most powerful steam locos on the Northern Counties Committee system. This example was built at the LMS Derby works.

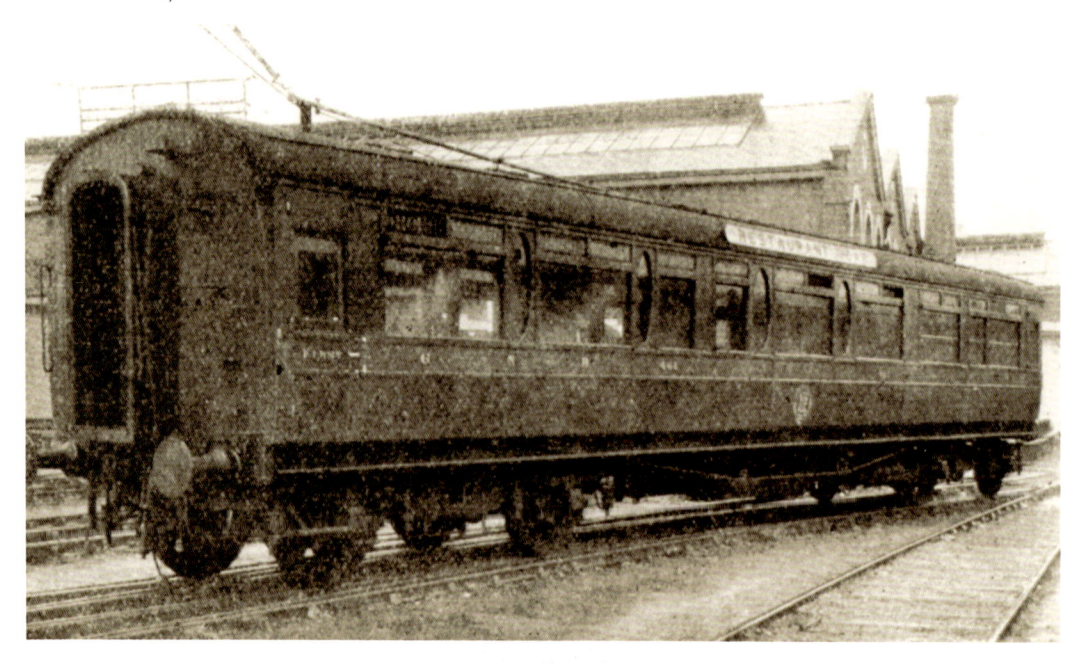

A restaurant car owned by the Great Northern railway. The company claimed to have been the first in the British Isles to have all its passenger rolling-stock electrically lit, and the first line to run restaurant cars in connection with sporting events.

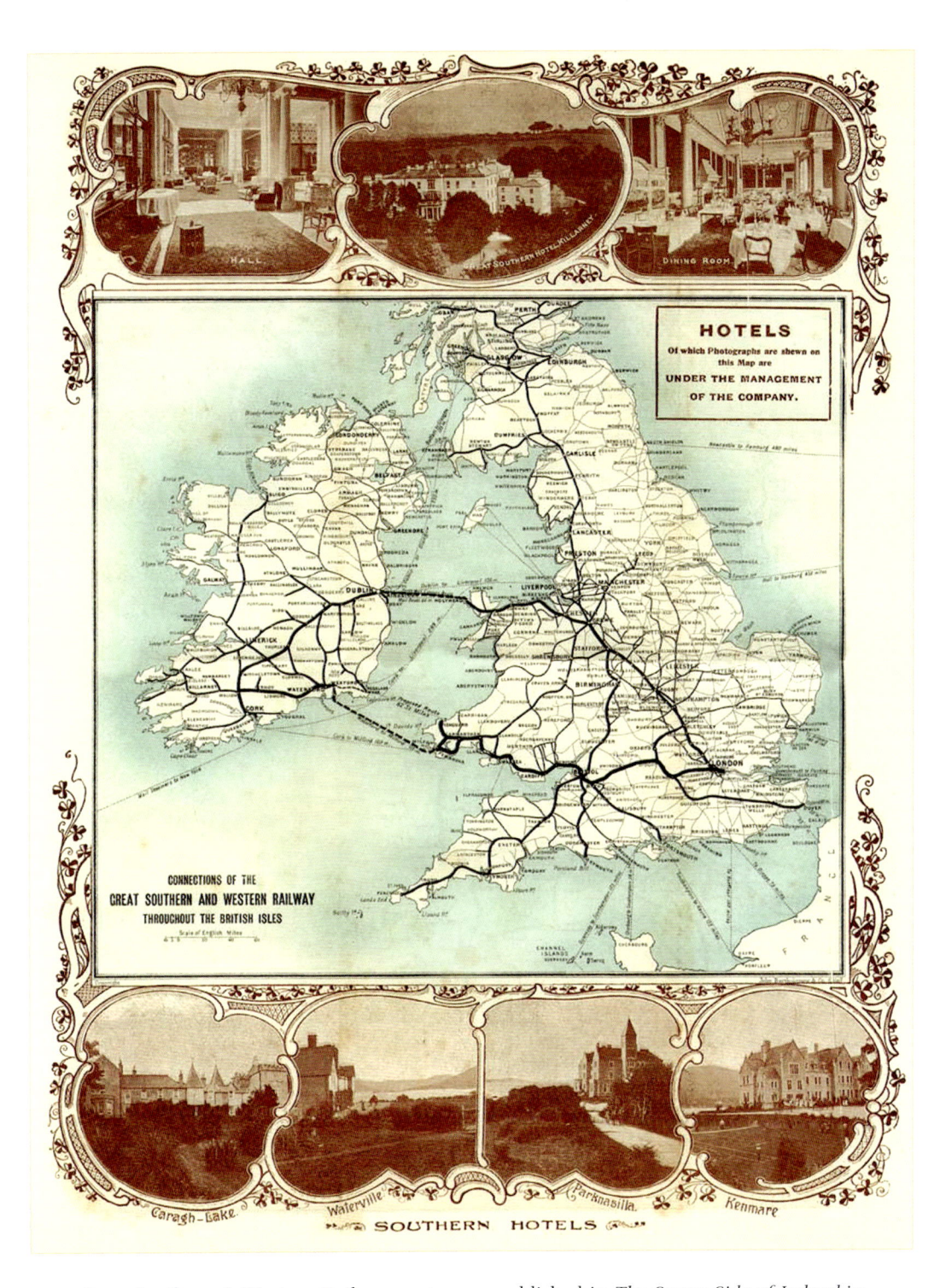

Great Southern & Western Railway route map published in *The Sunny Side of Ireland* in 1902. It includes hotels under the management of the company.

35

36

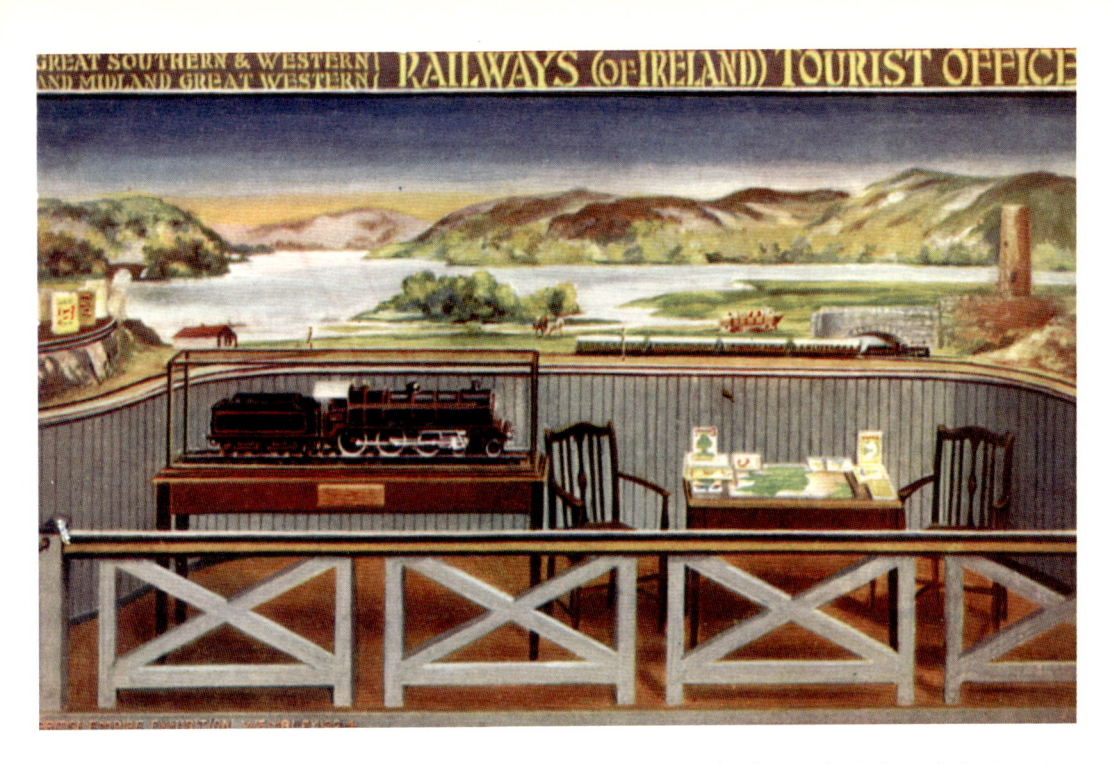

Great Southern & Western and the Midland Great Western display at the Palace of Engineering in the Wembley Exhibition held in London in 1924.

Advertising card for the Ireland to Holyhead service. *(J&C McCutcheon Collection)*

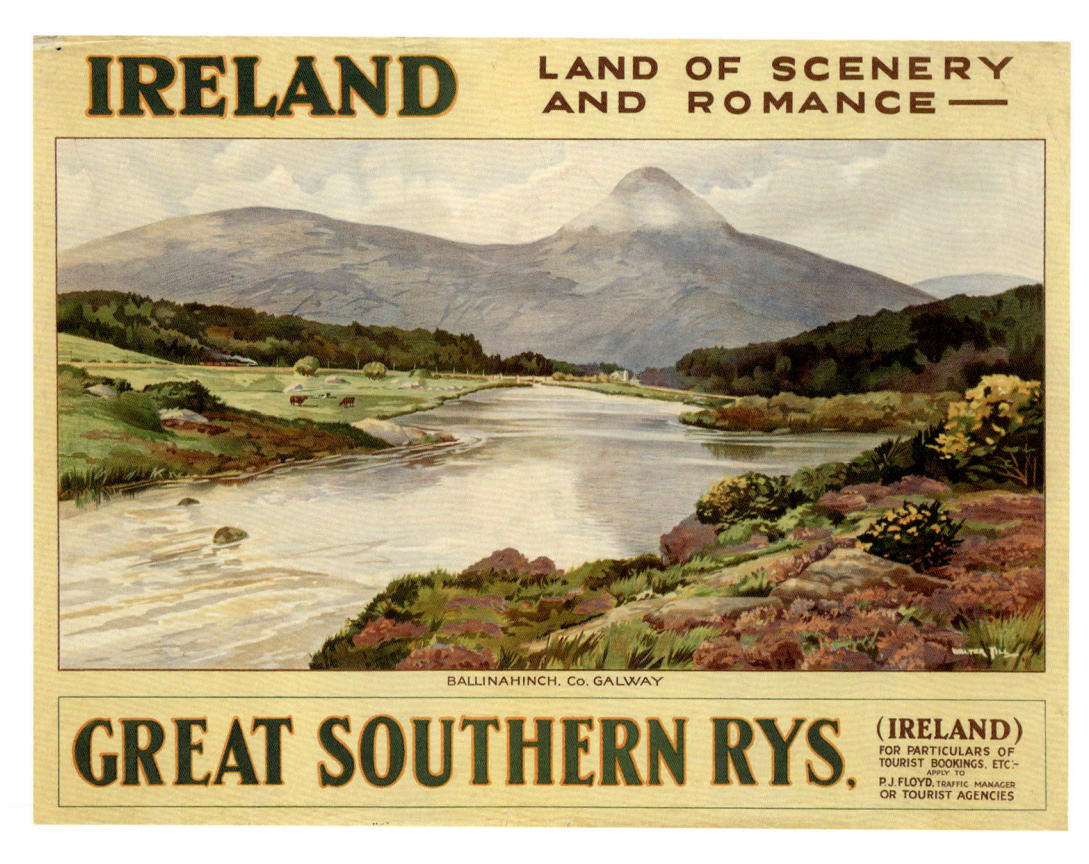

Two travel posters issued by the Great Southern Railways. 'Ireland – Land of Scenery and Romance' and 'Kilarney – Heaven's Reflex'.

KILLARNEY
Heaven's Reflex
GREAT SOUTHERN RYS
(IRELAND)
FOR PARTICULARS OF TOURIST BOOKINGS, ETC., APPLY TO:-
P. J. FLOYD, TRAFFIC MANAGER, OR TOURIST AGENCIES.
KINGSBRIDGE STATION, DUBLIN.
W.H. MORTON, GENERAL MANAGER.
For Travel Information and Illustrated Literature apply to Associated British Railways, Inc., 551 Fifth Avenue, New York, or Your Own Tourist Agent.

Cork Kent station
The wonderfully cluttered station platform at Cork Kent with a bewildering multiplicity of signage. Note the signs for the Ladies First Class Room and the ladies Third Class Room. The dark lines above the tracks and following their curve are shields to protect the glass roof from the blast of the chimney stacks as trains pull away. Date is around 1893, the year in which the stationed was opened by the GS&WR under its original name Glanmire Road station. *(National Library of Ireland/wiki)*

No. 36, a 3-foot gauge 2-2-2 locomotive built for the Great Southern Railways in 1848 and remained in service until 1874. The driving wheels are 6 feet in diameter, and this veteran loco was exhibited at the Cork Exhibition in 1902 and at the railway centenary celebrations at Stockton & Darlington in 1925. Since 2007 it has been on display on the concourse of the Cork Kent station. *(Andrew Abbott)*

Limerick station
The station on Parnell St was built by the Waterford & Limerick Railway and opened in August 1858. In this photograph a variety of horse-drawn vehicles are coming and going. In the foreground the local children jostle for position in front of the camera among a smartly dressed group of women. Judging by the poster on the gate post they may have been to the International Exhibition held in Dublin from May to November 1907. The station was renamed as Limerick Colbert in 1966. *(National Library of Ireland/wiki)*

Waterford station
Platform bookstall at Waterford station, *c.* 1924. You have to love the news placards, especially the one for John Bull. 'Wanted: One Honest Politician.' *(National Library of Ireland/wiki)*

Waterford
Steam-powered digger at work on the new railway cutting at Waterford with Irish navvies at work on their home soil. The terminus of the Waterford Cork railway line was in Waterford South station in Bilberry until a new railway bridge was constructed across the Suir and allowing the station to move to the present Waterford station site in 1905. The old line in Bilberry is now part of the Waterford – Kilmeaden tourist line. Note the makeshift points in the foreground. *(National Library of Ireland/wiki)*

Mitchell Brothers Contractors' locomotive No. 4, a small Manning Wardle & Co. 'H' class 0-4-0 saddle tank, in Waterford, south eastern Ireland, August 1905. *(National Library of Ireland/wiki)*

Troops depart from the Great Western Railway's Adelphi Quay in Waterford. An undated photograph, possibly from 1914. *(National Library of Ireland/wiki)*

45

Railway station at Athboy, County Meath on the eastern side of Ireland, *c.* 1900. The station master, bowler-hatted and standing beside the engine, is checking his watch. Athboy station opened in 1864, but was closed to the public in 1947 and closed for good in 1954. *(National Library of Ireland/wiki)*

Soldiers waiting for their train at Newbridge station in County Kildare, *c.* 1910. The Newbridge barracks was nearby, on the main street, but after Independence the new Irish Free State army chose not to retain it in favour of the barracks in Kildare, Naas and Curragh. *(National Library of Ireland/wiki)*

Station at Maynooth, County Kildare, 1962. The station is on the south side of the Royal Canal. *(National Library of Ireland/wiki)*

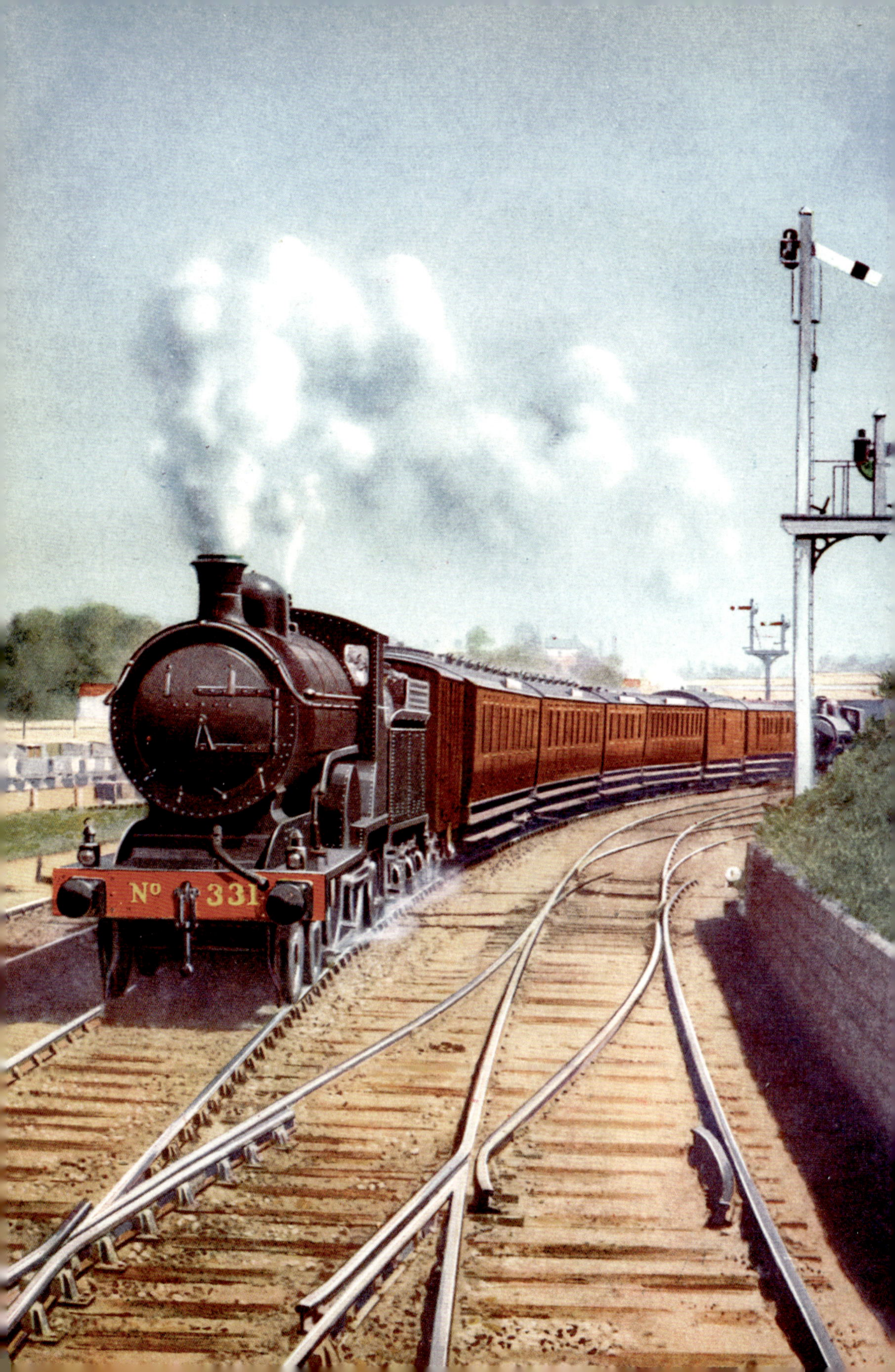
No 331

D&B steam tram
Above: An unusual push-me-pull-you Dublin & Blessington (D&B No. 2) steam tram, a double-cabbed 2-4-2 built by T. Green & Son Ltd. Of Leeds & London. The maker's plate shows No. 867. The trams operated between Terenure in Dublin and Blessington in County Wicklow, from 1888 until 1932. *(National Library of Ireland/wiki)*

Opposite: A Great Southern Railways passenger train, hauled by a 4-4-0 express loco, shown after departure from the Kingsbridge terminus in Dublin. Colour illustration from *Railway Wonders of the World*.

Dublin
Kingsbridge station was the main Dublin terminus of the Great Southern Railways. In 1925 all of the lines within the Irish Free State were amalgamated into the one enterprise, the GSR. At that time the company operated 2,157 miles of 5-foot 3-inch track.

Footbridge over the line at Churchdown, Dublin. January 1959. *(National Library of Ireland/wiki)*

Great Western Railways, No. 42 being cleaned in the train shed at Broadstone in Dublin. This was an Ivatt-designed 4-4-0 built in 1893 and designated as Class F6. It was withdrawn in 1963, the last of the class in use at that time. *(National Library of Ireland/wiki)*

Above: Locomotive No. 74 at the Cashel (Cahir) railway station, at the foot of the Rock of Cashel, South Tipperary. The Cashel Extension Railway arrived in October 1904 and to save money the buildings are of a very simple corrugated-iron construction. Judging by the freshness of the ballast and soil banks beside the line, this photograph must have been taken soon after the station opened. *(National Library of Ireland/wiki)*

Left: Driver Tom Crowe at Thurles Railway station, County Tipperary, July 1961. *(National Library of Ireland/wiki)*

The signal cabin at Athlone Wesy in County Westmeath. *(National Library Ireland/wiki)*

Tokens, sometimes referred to as staffs, in the signal box at Clonsilla, on the Dublin–Sligo line, County Dublin. The tokens ensure that only one train can run on a section of single track. The tokens are dispensed via the apparatus, which requires the signalmen at each end of the line to press buttons at the same time, and handed to the train's crew. Further tokens cannot be issued until the one in use is returned and replaced at the other end. *(National Library of Ireland/wiki)*

Valencia Harbour station
Next stop America! Locomotive No. 107, a coupled 0-6-0, at Valencia or Valentia Harbour station in County Kerry. Valentia is one of the Ireland's most westerly points and at Telegraph Field a monument marks the spot where the first transatlantic cable established a communications link between Europe and Heart's Content in Newfoundland, USA. The railway station was on the Great Southern & Western Railway which ran from Farrenfore and the harbour was a packet station for transatlantic liners from September 1893. The station closed in 1960. *(National Library of Ireland/wiki)*

Killarney
The Great Southern Railways' terminus at Killarney, County Kerry. The station opened in 1853, and to encourage tourism the GS&WR opened a hotel on the site, the first Railway-owned hotel in Ireland. *(National Library of Ireland/wiki)*

Colour postcard of the Royal Victoria Hotel Autobus in County Kerry. 'Linking railway and Killarney Lakes – 4 minute run.' *(J&C McCutcheon Collection)*

Newport
Workers pose in the mouth of the newly completed railway tunnel at Newport, County Mayo in the West Region of Ireland. The carved date stone says 1892. *(National Library of Ireland/wiki)*

A motor-bus operated by the Midland Great Western Railway, on the Castlebar road from Newport, County Mayo. *(National Library of Ireland/wiki)*

A load of Ford Prefect cars – the biggest selling car in Ireland at one time – a single Thames van, at Claremorris station in County Mayo. Photographed from the footbridge. The Irish railways built up a substantial freight service, partly because of the state of the roads. These shiny and unregistered cars have come from the Ford works at Cork. This was the first purpose-built Ford factory in Europe and originally turned out the Fordson tractors. This photograph was taken in September 1950. *(National Library of Ireland/wiki)*

Left: The demolition of Clones station, County Monaghan, photographed in November 1960 by James O'Dea. *(National Library of Ireland/wiki)*

Below: A goods train climbing a bank of 1 in 40 on the Northern Counties Committee line. The train is hauled by a 2-4-2 compound engine.

Off to the races
Smartly-dressed race-goers pour out of the train at Laytown station in County Meath, eastern Ireland, *c.* 1910. They are off to the Laytown Races. The station opened in 1844 and was renamed Laytown & Bettystown in 1913. *(National Library of Ireland/wiki)*

End of the line
Cavan & Leitrim Railway workshop at Ballinamore, showing redundant locomotives being cut up. This 3-foot narrow gauge line in the northwest of Ireland opened in 1887. The line was amalgamated with the Great Southern Railways in 1925 and continued to run until March 1959. It was the last exclusively narrow gauge line in Ireland. *(National Library of Ireland/wiki)*

Cavan & Leitrim Railway
Lifting the tracks at Garadice, County Leitrim, in July 1959.
The line was built by the Cavan & Leitrim Railway. *(National Library of Ireland/wiki)*

The preserved Cavan & Leitrim Railway depot at Dromod in County Antrim, 2007. Run by volunteers, the narrow gauge trains continue to run every weekend and on Mondays. *(Sarah777)*

Boyne Viaduct, Drogheda

The Boyne Viaduct at Drogheda
Once carrying the Great Northern Railway's main line from Dublin and Belfast over the River Boyne, the viaduct was designed by the Irish engineer, Sir John MacNeill, and completed in 1855. Postcard, c. 1905. *(J&C McCutcheon Collection)* The bridge was refurbished in the 1930s with new steel girders replacing the straight iron-girder sections. In addition the two tracks were reduced to one. The recent photograph is from 2007. *(Trounce)*

Rail-bus
The 'Rail Omnibus' was a pneumatic-tyred vehicle on the Great Northern Railway. The wheels have steel rims between the rubber tyres and the rails. The advantage claimed for this system was that the rail omnibus could stop at level crossings and pick up passengers at any point. This offered the potential for economical services in the more thinly-populated districts.

64

Diesel rail car
One of four diesel rail cars built in 1932 at the Dundalk works for service on the Great Northern Railway. The interior was plain but comfortable.

Northern Counties Committee rail-cars were introduced for light suburban work. They were fitted with two Leyland Diesel engines, each developing 130 brake horse-power at 2,000 revolutions per minute.

Diesel railcar No. 4, built by the Northern Counties Committee Company at York Road works in 1938. Photographed at York Road station, Belfast, in September 1959 with members of the Irish Railway Record Society about to board the special to Cookstown Junction and Kilrea. *(National Library of Ireland/wiki)*

Electric
An electrically-powered train passing through Lucan station, County Dublin. It was operated using the quick-charging Drumm Traction Battery on the Great Southern Railways suburban trains. During trial runs in 1932 the Drumm train accelerated to 50 mph within 50 seconds of starting.

67

The Latrigue Monorail
Ireland's most unusual railway was the Behr monorail which ran between Listowel and Ballybunion in County Kerry. Opened in 1888 it used the Latrigue Monorail system developed by the French engineer Charles Latrigue. The special locomotive was built by the Hunslet company and hauled double sided passenger carriages on an A-shaped trestle. At the junction a section of rail was swung aside like a gate to let the trains through. Only two trains, one each way, ran every day. The line closed in 1924 after the track was deliberately damaged. It reopened in 2003 and is now run by the Latrigue Monorail Restoration committee, worked by a diesel built to resemble the original steam loco.

Junction on the monorail, top., and signalman in action on the line in 1888.

Belfast
Great Northern Railway station in Belfast, *c.* 1900. *(National Library of Ireland/wiki)*

Although the main Irish gauge was 5 feet 3 inches, the Northern Counties Committee had 64 miles of 3-foot track, in addition to 201 miles of the broad gauge. This is a narrow-gauge 2-4-2 compound loco on a broad-gauge transhipment truck in Belfast. The initials 'MR' stand for Midland railway, later absorbed within the LMS), which acquired the Belfast and Northern Counties Railway in 1903.

York Road station, also referred to as Belfast York Road station, was formerly one of the three termini in the city. Originally opened in April 1848 as a modest structure for the Belfast & Ballymena Railway, and a major rebuild in the 1890s saw the addition of the clock tower. The York Road closed in 1992 and no traces of the station remain. *(National Library of Ireland/wiki)*

The North Atlantic Express of the Northern Counties Committee (LMS) system leaving Belfast. This express provided a daily service between Belfast and Portrush, a distance of 65 miles which it covered in 80 minutes. These corridor coaches were built in the NCC's workshops.

The Egyptian Arch
Mc Neill's Egyptian Arch at Newry, County Down in Northern Ireland, *c.* 1905. It was completed in 1851 for the Dublin & Belfast Junction Railway. It is thought that this photograph was taken by Robert French, chief photographer of William Lawrence photographic Studios of Dublin. The Egyptian style was very popular in the mid-nineteenth century and was much favoured by the engineer Isambard Kingdom Brunel for his Clifton Suspension Bridge in Bristol. *(National Library of Ireland/wiki)*

Portadown
An early photograph of the wide frontage of Portadown Station, County Armagh in Northern Ireland, c. 1879. The original station was half a mile to the east and opened in 1842. It has since moved location several times. Note the gentleman posting up stickers on the gate piers despite the sign that says 'Post No Bills'. *(National Library of Ireland/wiki)*

Carnlough
The viaduct at Carnlough in County Antrim in Northern Ireland, c. 1900. The town hall is on the right and the post office is also on the right just beyond, and hidden by, the viaduct. But note the mysterious headless train driver. *(National Library of Ireland/wiki)*

LMS NORTHERN IRELAND
by Hesketh Hubbard V-P.R.B.A.R.O.I.

Great Southern and Western Railway Co's Hotel, Waterville, Co. Kerry.

Above: Postcard of the Northern Counties Hotel in Portrush. *(J&C McCutcheon Collection)*

Opposite top: LMS poster for Northern Ireland.

Opposite bottom: A fantastic setting for the Great Southern & Western Railway's hotel at Waterville, County Derry. *(J&C McCutcheon Collection)*

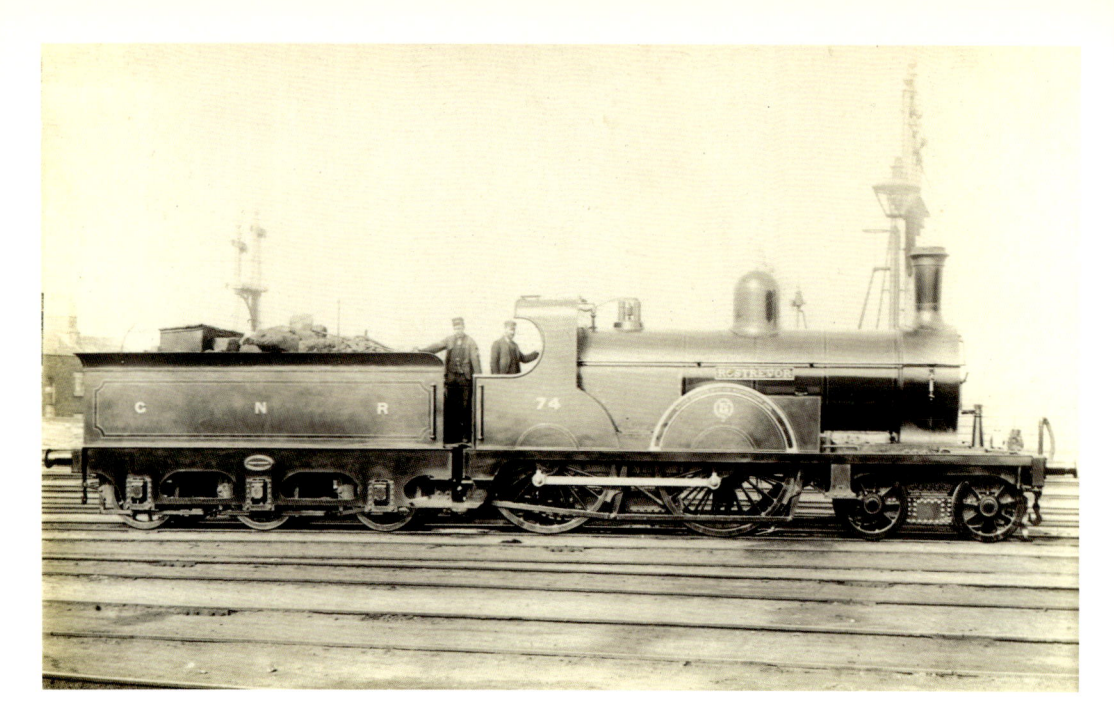

Above: GNR PP class No. 74, *Rostrevor*, a 4-4-0 built in 1896 by Beyer Peacock. Several rebuilds and finally withdrawn in 1963. *Below:* Enniskillen train. *(J&C McCutcheon Collection)*

Above: 0-6-0, No. 709. *Below:* 4-4-0 No. 174, *Carrantuohill*, near Portadown. *(J&C McCutcheon Collection)*

IRELAND
· GEM OF THE SEA ·

THE BOG ROAD.

GREAT SOUTHERN RAILWAYS

Ireland – Gem of the Sea
Cover of a guide book published by the Great Southern Railways, Kingsbridge Station, Dublin, 1935. Similar publications were produced by many of the railway companies, and this describes some of the attractions within their area. The following pages, including the advertisements for the railway company's hotel, are taken from this guide book. *(J&C McCutcheon Collection)*

TOURING FOR HEALTH AND PLEASURE

ON

Great Southern Railways
(IRELAND)

TRANSPORT SERVICES.

Tourist and Summer Excursion Tickets are issued by Railway during the Season to the Tourist and Seaside Resorts in the
IRISH FREE STATE

Full information respecting Railway services and fares may be obtained on application to P. J. Floyd, Traffic Manager, Kingsbridge, Dublin; respecting omnibus services and fares to R. D. Griffith, Manager, Bus Dept., Transport House, Bachelor's Walk, Dublin, and in regard to all facilities from GREAT SOUTHERN RAILWAYS INFORMATION BUREAU, 33 BACHELOR'S WALK, DUBLIN; T. R. Dester, Assoc., British Railways Inc., 551 Fifth Av., New York; or to any of the Railways' appointed Tourist Agents

W. H. MORTON
General Manager

Kingsbridge Station
Dublin, 1935

This Guide is published by the GREAT SOUTHERN RAILWAYS (IRELAND), revised by W. H. BRAYDEN and printed in Ireland by BROWNE AND NOLAN, LTD. Nassau Street, Dublin

YOUGHAL (CO. CORK)	**ESPLANADE HOTEL, FRONT STRAND.** On the Promenade. Fully licensed. Moderate charges. Electric light and fires throughout. Radio. Free garage. Hot salt water and sea-weed baths. The Management endeavours to provide all home comforts.
YOUGHAL	**YOUGHAL HOTEL, GREEN PARK.** The largest and leading first-class Hotel. Beautifully situated in its own grounds, overlooking the sea. Renovated throughout. Tennis, fishing, shooting, Fully licensed. Garage. Telephone No. 6. Telegrams, "Ledingham." M. J. LEDINGHAM, Proprietor.

GREAT SOUTHERN RAILWAYS

"ALL IN" TOURS.

These Tours have been compiled so as to enable the Tourist to visit the most delightful scenery and spend happy holidays at a reasonable cost.

The charges quoted for the Tours enumerated provide on an economical basis—Travel Tickets, Hotel Accommodation, consisting of Bedroom, Meat Breakfast, Luncheon and Evening Dinner.

FARE FROM DUBLIN

	1st Class Throughout	3rd Cl. Rail 1st Grade Hotel	3rd Cl. Rail 2nd Grade Hotel
	£ s. d.	£ s. d.	£ s. d.
A Week in the South	11 10 6	10 12 6	9 11 6
A Week in the West	7 15 6	7 1 0	—
A Week in Connemara	7 3 0	6 10 6	—
8 Days in Wicklow and the South	13 1 0	12 1 0	10 19 0
8 Days in the South and West	13 5 0	12 4 6	11 10 3
11 Days in Wicklow, the South and West	16 15 0	15 18 0	14 13 3
8 Days in Cashel, Limerick, Cork, Glengarriff, Killarney	12 17 3	12 0 0	10 18 3
11 Days Grand Tour of the Irish Free State	17 1 0	16 0 0	15 0 6
11 Days in the West, Clare and the South	17 1 3	16 0 6	14 18 6

For particulars of these and other Tours apply to—

P. J. FLOYD, *Traffic Manager.*

KINGSBRIDGE STATION, DUBLIN.

INTRODUCTION.

THE attractions of Ireland as a tourist centre and the best place in which to spend a happy holiday, have been described, especially in recent years, by many eloquent writers. Their best encomium has been the accounts of those visitors who have come to our shores, and gone away delighted with their experiences. The year 1932 brought to Ireland enormous numbers for the Eucharistic Congress. Never before has there been such an influx of visitors from so many countries making their acquaintance with the beauties of all parts of Ireland. To some their visit was a great adventure, and it may even have appeared as something of a risk, for the Ireland of the world's newspapers has small resemblance to the Ireland we know. The main impression of the pilgrim was one of surprise and pleasure. Our visitors were prepared for the beauty of Irish scenery, which has few rivals anywhere for its charm and variety. It is not, however, from the impressive scenery alone that the pleasure from a visit arises—no!—the opportunities for healthful sport, fishing and golf, the excellence of the roads, especially the main roads, for motoring, the ease and unexpectedness of the ways of Irish life, make an Irish tour an experience to be treasured in the memory. The facilities, and general cheapness, of travel throughout the country, have been universally praised by hundreds who came expecting something primitive, and found instead modern efficiency and comfort. Ireland has had a reputation in the past of being rather " easy going "—yet it has exhibited to the world a capacity for organisation by the provision of comfortable accommodation for unprecedented numbers, and there has been a remarkable absence of any complaints. Ireland afforded a glorious example to the world in that memorable year. Moreover, it made itself better known to Irishmen and Irishwomen at home, thousands of whom learned of the possibilities of finding within its borders pleasures of travel and change of scene that they had previously sought abroad.

The Irish Tourist Associations have done excellent service to all tourists, home and foreign, and have helped to raise the comfort and efficiency of hotels all over the country, and to standardise their charges, so that the visitor can find acceptable accommodation at the price he is prepared to pay. Accommodation, of course, varies in proportion to requirements, yet the general experience now is that the visitor gets full value for what he spends, and that there are no surprises on the bills. The Great Southern Railways Company's Hotels, including those at such notable resorts as Killarney, Kenmare, Parknasilla, Galway, Mallaranny and Sligo, admittedly rival successfully, in the comforts they supply and the reasonableness of their charge for them, the standard of first class hotels anywhere. The Great Southern Railways Company, which covers The Free State with a network of Railway lines of over 2,000 miles, and passenger road omnibus services of over 3,800 miles of road that enables travellers by the combined use of Railway and road services to reach places of interest off the beaten track—all over the country, has provided cheap tickets in connection with their Hotels, combining the charge for Rail transit and that for hotel accommodation at the most reasonable rates.

For Dublin the great week is Horse Show Week, the first week in August in each year. It brings together always a microcosm of Irish life in all its aspects, as well as many visitors from abroad. The figures of attendance on its four days run from 90,000

CHAMBER OF DEPUTIES, DÁIL ÉIREANN

DUN LAOGHAIRE, CO. DUBLIN

BRAY HEAD AND BEACH, CO. WICKLOW

ENNISKERRY, CO. WICKLOW

to 100,000. Nearly 1,000 Irish hunters are on exhibition every year and the jumping competitions, especially the military international competitions between the officers of European armies, for the cup presented by the Aga Khan, are an unfailing attraction. In conjunction with the Show are " the Sales," where yearlings for which Ireland is famed are shown. In the past animals bought at the Show have become world famous by winning the chief classical races in England. In the Show grounds are 10,000 available reserved seats which yearly are eagerly booked.

Ireland offers many attractions to the motorist. Much money has been spent on the improvement of the roads. It has been frequently stated by visitors that the main roads are on the whole better than those in Great Britain, while, avoiding comparison, all are agreed that the main roads can truly be described as " excellent." Of course the quality of the surface varies in different districts, and though the side roads in Ireland, as in most countries, leave something to be desired, there is an advantage in the absence of congestion, and the motorist is not made to feel that he is one in a long procession. Garages, petrol pumps, and so forth are to be found at frequent intervals even in remote districts. Some people may be deterred by the fear of difficulties with the Customs. But the genuine tourists will find all these difficulties smoothed away by the Automobile Association, whose triptychs are familiar all over Ireland. It is the testimony not only of motorists but of all tourists that the Customs Officials of the Free State, though a new force, are courteous, helpful and reasonable.

There are plenty of good golf links. Dublin has some famous ones, and no considerable centre of population is without at least one. The hotels facilitate the sport. Nearly 200 clubs make up the Golfing Union of Ireland, and visitors are welcomed.

Mr. Stephen Gwynn, the Irish essayist, novelist and poet, is an enthusiastic fisherman, and to him, as he says in his delightful and informing kitbag travel book on " Ireland," " Ireland's extraordinary attraction is the range and variety of fishing it offers all the year round. There is water everywhere and all the fresh water holds fish ; most of it holds trout and salmon and sea-trout and a vast deal of it is free." In other directions also the country provides abundantly for the devotees of sport, whether it be on the racing track —or amongst the gorse—gun in hand, or else in the off season joining in that fine sport—hunting, facilities for which exist in almost every county.

The Company is always willing and most anxious to assist visitors by forwarding on application information in regard to fare facilities and to advise in regard to choice of Holiday Resorts, or else to plan whole tours of the country.

The photographs of the illustrations appearing in this book have been supplied through the courtesy of Mr. T. H. Mason, 5 and 6 Dame Street, Dublin.

Great Southern Railways' Omnibus Department
ROAD MOTOR TOURS
In Luxurious Sunshine Coaches
JUNE TO SEPTEMBER INCLUSIVE

NINE DAY TOUR ..	..	£13 0 0
SEVEN DAY TOUR	..	£10 0 0
SIX DAY TOUR ..	..	£7 7 0

Fares include first-class Hotel accommodation and gratuities. A Guide accompanies each Tour. Tourists are met on arrival at Boat or Railway Station and conveyed to Hotel or to starting point of Tour and on completion of Tour will be conveyed to Hotel, Boat or Station, free of extra charge.

City Sight Seeing Tour of Dublin, Whole-Day and Half-Day trips to Glendalough, Liffey Valley Tour, Surprise Tours afternoon and evening.

Brochure of Tours giving full particulars may be had on application to Travel Agents or to this Office.

D'Olier House, D'Olier Street,　　　　**W. H. MORTON,**
　　Dublin, C.5.　　　　　　　　　　　General Manager.
　　　　　　'Phones : 43147/8.

ACROSS THE STREET or ACROSS THE WORLD

Express Parcels Delivery

Great Southern Railways
ROAD FREIGHT
and
CARTAGE DEPARTMENT

Furniture Removals Storages

BACHELOR'S WALK, DUBLIN

IRELAND

THE EMERALD ISLE

Rail and Sea Connections with GREAT BRITAIN

🍀

Via HOLYHEAD and DÚN LAOGHAIRE (Kingstown)

THE London, Midland and Scottish Railway Company's principal route to and from the Irish Free State is via Holyhead and Dun Laoghaire (Kingstown). The "Irish Mail" which traverses this route has for nearly 100 years carried His Majesty's Mails between London and Dublin, and runs every day via Crewe and Chester to Holyhead, and thence to Dun Laoghaire (Kingstown). It is equipped with

First and Third Class Restaurant Cars by day and First and Third Class Sleeping Accommodation by night.

Passengers step off the train at Holyhead alongside a luxuriously equipped modern Turbine Steamer of 3,450 tons, with a speed of 25 knots—an Atlantic Liner in miniature. The open sea passage is only 2¾ hours. There are two services each way every week-day; a night service only on Sundays.

Via FISHGUARD and ROSSLARE.

THE Great Western Railway's principal route to and from Ireland is via Fishguard and Rosslare, and there is a service in both directions each week-day, with train connections from Paddington, Plymouth, Bath, Bristol, Birmingham, Oxford, Cheltenham, Gloucester, Newport, Cardiff, Swansea, etc.

Trains run alongside the Steamers at Fishguard and Rosslare, and

First and Third Class Sleeping Accommodation,

as well as

Restaurant Cars,

are provided on the Boat Trains between Fishguard and Paddington.

HOW TO SEE IRELAND!

Let COOK'S advise you. They know the best ways to see the choicest spots. They will plan your itinerary and arrange your journey ahead without extra charge. They will reserve your hotel accommodation in advance and look after your sight-seeing expeditions.

The Illustrated Booklet

"HOW TO SEE IRELAND"

will give you useful information about the places you particularly want to see. Copy free from any office of

THOS. COOK & SON, LTD.

(Official Agents for Great Southern Railways)

BERKELEY ST., LONDON, W.1. And 350 Offices including

DUBLIN:	BELFAST:	CORK Agent:
118 Grafton St.	27 Royal Avenue.	J. Barter & Sons, 9 Patrick St.

TRAVEL to IRELAND

7 ROUTES

FISHGUARD to CORK—Direct
Leave Paddington *5.55 p.m. Tues., Thurs. and Sats.

LIVERPOOL to DUBLIN
Leave Euston *6.5 p.m. Nightly (Sundays excepted).

LIVERPOOL to BELFAST
Leave Euston *6.5 p.m. Nightly (Sundays excepted).

ARDROSSAN to BELFAST
Royal Mail Route. Leave Glasgow (Central) 10.30 p.m. (St. Enoch), 9.20 p.m. Nightly (Saturdays and Sundays excepted).

GLASGOW to BELFAST—DIRECT
Leave Glasgow 9.0 p.m. (Saturdays 10.45 p.m.) Nightly (Sundays excepted).

GLASGOW & GREENOCK to DUBLIN
Four or more Sailings Every Week.

GLASGOW & GREENOCK to DERRY
Four or more Sailings Every Week.

* Restaurant Boat Express.

TRAVEL by the NEW SHIPS

YOUR ROUTES

BETWEEN

ENGLAND & IRELAND

ARE THE

ROYAL MAIL ROUTES

The Great Western Route via Fishguard and Rosslare.				The London, Midland and Scottish Route via Holyhead and Kingstown.			
SERVICE TO IRELAND				**SERVICE TO IRELAND**			
			Week-days p.m.			Week-days a.m.	p.m.
LONDON (Paddington)	...	dep.	7.55	LONDON (Euston)	dep.	8.45	8.45
BIRMINGHAM (Snow Hill)	...	,,	6.30	BIRMINGHAM (New St.)	,,	9.45	10.15
GLOUCESTER	...	,,	8.15	LIVERPOOL (Lime Street)	,,	10.55	10.45
BRISTOL (Temple Meads)	...	,,	8.55	MANCHESTER (Exchange)	,,	11.0	10.20
FISHGUARD HARBOUR	...	,,	a.m. 2.10	HOLYHEAD	,,	p.m. 2.30	a.m. 2.55
ROSSLARE HARBOUR	...	arr.	5.25	DUN LAOGHAIRE (Kingstown Pier)	arr.	5.25	5.50

Convenient services are also given from other principal towns to Ireland; and services also operate from Ireland to all parts of Great Britain.

The trains of the Great Southern Railways Company of Ireland connect with the Steamers at Rosslare and Kingstown.

Illustrated Guide to Holiday Resorts and information respecting Passenger and Goods Services between Great Britain and Ireland on application to

G.W. Railway, Paddington. L.M.S. Railway, Euston.
G.S. Railways, Dublin.

GREAT SOUTHERN HOTEL

KILLARNEY (100 Rooms)

This Hotel is the largest and best appointed in the Lake District. Situated in its own ornamental grounds. It is an excellent centre for Motorists. Garage attached to the Hotel.

Central Heating, Electric Light. Hot and Cold Water in Bedrooms.

Nine-Hole Golf Course convenient. Coaching and Boating excursions arranged daily.

Hotel Porters meet all Trains for conveyance of luggage.

Tariff is Moderate,
and can be had on application to the Manageress.

'Phone : Killarney 26.   Telegrams—" Railway Hotel, Killarney."

PADDY

PURE POT STILL WHISKY
TEN YEARS OLD
DISTILLED, MATURED, and BOTTLED BY
CORK DISTILLERIES CO., LTD.
CORK.

IRELAND
Land of Romance
Blarney Castle Co Cork
GREAT SOUTHERN RYS.
(IRELAND)
FOR PARTICULARS OF TOURIST BOOKINGS ETC.
APPLY TO:- P. J. FLOYD - TRAFFIC MANAGER
OR TOURIST AGENCIES
KINGSBRIDGE STATION DUBLIN.
W. H. MORTON. GENERAL MANAGER.

Acknowledgements

The images in this book have come from a number of sources: The National Library of Ireland (wiki commons), the J&C McCutcheon Collection, the US Library of Congress, Boston Public Library, Sarah777, Andrew Abbott, Trounce and other contemporary sources including *Railway Wonders of the World* and publicity material of the Great Southern Railways.

Opposite: Great Southern Railways poster, 'Ireland – Land of Romance', with an illustration of Blarney Castle, County Cork.

LONDONDERRY
THE
NORTH-WEST OF IRELAND
THE DONEGAL RAILWAY COMPANY
TYRCONNEL
DONEGAL "THE LAND OF TYRCONNEL" BY
THE DONEGAL RAILWAY Co.
LOUGH ESKE
DONEGAL CASTLE
SLIEVE LEAGUE
BARNESMORE GAP
ALL INFORMATION FROM MR. R.H. LIVESEY GENERAL MANAGER. STRANORLAR. CO. DONEGAL.